D0337402

Unity (1918)

Unity (1918)

Kevin Kerr

Talonbooks
2002

Copyright © 2002 Kevin Kerr

Talonbooks
P.O. Box 2076, Vancouver, British Columbia, Canada V6B 3S3
www.talonbooks.com

Typeset in New Baskerville and printed and bound in Canada.

Third Printing: July 2003

No part of this book, covered by the copyright hereon, may be repro-
duced or used in any form or by any means—graphic, electronic or
mechanical—without prior permission of the publisher, except for
excerpts in a review. Any request for photocopying of any part of this
book shall be directed in writing to Cancopy (Canadian Copyright
Licensing Agency), 1 Yonge Street Suite 1900, Toronto, Ontario,
Canada M5E 1E5; Tel.:(416) 868-1620; Fax:(416) 868-1621.

Rights to produce *Unity (1918)*, in whole or in part, in any medium
by any group, amateur or professional, are retained by the author.
Interested persons are requested to apply to him c/o Talonbooks,
P.O. Box 2076, Vancouver, BC V6B 3S3; tel: (604) 444-4889, fax:
(604) 444-4119.

National Library of Canada Cataloguing in Publication Data

Kerr, Kevin, 1968-
  Unity (1918)

  A play.
  ISBN 0-88922-461-7

  I. Title.
PS8571.E719U54 2002   C812'.6   C2002-910063-1
PR9199.4.K47U54 2002

The publisher gratefully acknowledges the financial support of the
Canada Council for the Arts; the Government of Canada through the
Book Publishing Industry Development Program; and the Province
of British Columbia through the British Columbia Arts Council for
our publishing activities.

In memory of
Violet Kezia Markusson
1915–1999

Unity (1918) was developed as part of Touchstone Theatre's Playwright in Residence Program during the 1999/2000 season, and was first produced by that company in March 2001 at the Vancouver East Cultural Centre in Vancouver, B.C. with the following cast and production team:

BEATRICE. . . . . Michelle Porter
SISSY . . . . Dawn Petten
SUNNA. . . . . Kerry Sandomirsky
HART . . . . Robert Moloney
MICHAEL / GLEN / MAN 2 . . . . Bob Frazer
MARY . . . . Sarah Louise Turner
ROSE. . . . . Wendy Morrow Donaldson
DORIS . . . . Gina Stockdale
STAN / MAN 1 / CHAPERONE . . . . . . David Bloom
Directed by Katrina Dunn
Set Design: Robert Gardiner
Costume Design: Mara Gottler
Lighting Design: Adrian Muir
Sound Design & Original Music: Patrick Pennefather
Stage Manager: Jessica Chambers

Unity (1918) was created through the generous support of the Canada Council for the Arts, B.C. Arts Council, Touchstone Theatre, Playwrights Theatre Centre, and was further developed at the Banff Centre *playRites 2000* playwrights colony.

Special thanks to dramaturge Elizabeth Dancoes for her invaluable input, support, and dedication; to Chapelle Jaffe at Playwrights Theatre Centre and Katrina Dunn at Touchstone who supported the project from such an early stage; and to Paul Lefebvre my dramaturge at Banff for his passion, wisdom, and belief in the play. Also huge thanks to all of the Markussons, my family in Saskatchewan who helped me with the research; to my parents for their encouragement; and to Marita for her love and support.

Characters:

BEATRICE, a farmer's daughter
SISSY, her younger sister, a doomsday prophet
MARY, a debutante, Beatrice's best friend
ROSE, a telephone operator
DORIS, a telegraph operator
SUNNA, a mortician and an outcast
STAN, an incompetent farmer and widower
HART, a blinded war hero
MICHAEL, a farm hand
GLEN, a returning war veteran
TWO MEN on the street, farmers
A CHAPERONE at the V-Day dance

Suggested doublings:
MICHAEL / GLEN / MAN 1
STAN / MAN 2 / Voice of CHAPERONE

Note on events:

In the fall of 1918 an influenza pandemic swept the planet. Largely forgotten now, this was the deadliest outbreak of an infectious virus in recorded history. Although it is uncertain exactly how many people died, estimates range from twenty to fifty million people worldwide. The flu reached every corner of the globe and was aided by the movements of troops at the tail end of World War I. It was an especially unusual strain of this otherwise common sickness, as the victims were mainly young adults twenty to forty years of age—strong and healthy and in the prime of life. In Canada, where per capita war casualties were particularly severe, more people died in four weeks of the flu than did in four years of fighting.

Unity is a town in Saskatchewan about an hour's drive west of Saskatoon. Although the story is based on certain specific events of the period, the characters and action depicted in the play are fictitious.

Note on punctuation and overlapping dialogue (*cf.* Caryl Churchill):

A slash mark ("/") marks the point in a character's line where the next character begins speaking.

Example:

SISSY: I don't have a / boyfriend.

HART: You got your man overseas?

(Here HART begins speaking on "have a")

If the line of dialogue with the "/" doesn't end with any punctuation mark ("." "?" "—" "...") it means that character keeps speaking on top of the other character's line through to their next line without break.

Example:

SISSY: I can fight. I could be that woman in the painting, / leading the

BEA: What painting?

SISSY: army, you know, where everybody's following her and she's carrying the flag over the hill, boobies hanging out of her dress and she doesn't even care.

(Here BEATRICE asks "What painting?" midstream, but SISSY doesn't pause for the question)

An asterisk ("*") at the end of a line indicates the cue for a character to speak who has an "*" at the beginning of her line, even though on the page a line or more of dialogue may separate the text of the first character from the response of the other.

Example:

HART: And it killed him?

SUNNA: Yes.*

HART: Shame.

BEA: *Oh my God! Who?

(Here SUNNA's line "Yes" serves as the cue for both HART and BEA's next line.)

An em dash ("—") marks a break or sudden shift in thought. At the end of a line it's a sudden stop or cut off. Within a line it's a sudden mental change of direction.

An ellipse ("...") indicates the speaker trails off or hesitates before continuing. Also, it may indicate a short pause between lines.

Prologue

Darkness. The sound of a threshing machine. A distant horrible roar. Lights slowly rise. BEATRICE writes in her diary.

BEA: October 15, 1918. Today I turned twenty-one and there was a party. Some would say small, but just right for me.

SISSY and MARY appear wearing party hats.

SIS & MARY: (*singing together*)

Happy Birthday To You …

BEA: Sister got back—just in time—from her trip to Edmonton with father. She said there were boys there—

SISSY: Lots of boys!

BEA: She said there were a group of boys from Ontario who had left to escape conscription and were heading north to Alaska to look for gold.
I said they were cowards.
Mary said they were traitors.
Sister said they were swell.

SISSY: They *were* swell!

BEA: Mary said,

MARY: I don't care about boys in Edmonton.

BEA: Then she read us a letter from Richard who's still in France. Richard says,

MARY: The war will be over soon.

BEA: Richard says,

MARY: We're going to win.

BEA: Richard says,

MARY: He killed a German with his bare hands!

BEA: Richard says,

MARY: He's now in bed with the flu and when he's better he's coming home.

BEA: And in the meantime he's imagining every nurse is Mary, who, he says,

MARY: Is prettier than all the nurses in France put together.

BEA: And sister said,

SISSY: Well, I should hope so, 'cause that would be one ugly monster with a thousand heads all spouting French—Mange, Mange, Mange!

BEA: And Richard says, when he comes home they will get married.

SISSY: Married?

MARY: Married!

SISSY and MARY shriek with delight.

BEA: I asked if he mentioned Glen.

MARY: Why?

BEA: Well, they're good friends and all.

MARY: No, he didn't.

BEA: Oh.
Sister brought back two books given to her by
one of the boys. One was a strange book, which
says that parts of the Bible reveal that the world
will come to an end *this* year! Sister is convinced
it's true.

SISSY: Look at the war! It's a sure sign itself. Millions
and millions of people have already died and
that's almost everybody!

MARY: That's scary.

BEA: The other was a book by an American woman on
a subject that I'm not sure I can bring myself to
write of, even in this most private of places.
Her message is that a woman can chose when she
might or mightn't have a baby, but never have to
abstain from being with her husband—and that
she may derive a great deal of pleasure ...
Mary read several passages aloud—one of which
described a wooden mechanical device for ...

MARY: Look there's a drawing!

SISSY: (*laughing*) Ew!

BEA: (*grabbing the book and slamming it shut*) Sissy! You
should throw this on the fire before anyone sees
it.

SISSY: I'll hide it.

Pause.

BEA: Where?

SISSY: Oh, don't worry Beatrice, you'll never have to
see it again.

BEA: I don't like what's becoming of my sister. Perhaps
the world is coming to an end.

Distance is growing between the girls.

BEA: P.S. Old Mr. Thorson, the undertaker, died today.
Due to drink I suppose. They say Sunna, his
niece, will perform his duties—at least for now.
Imagine!

MARY: A woman doing that!

SISSY: And she's only fifteen!

MARY: But somehow she looks twice that.

BEA: A strange pair they were.
Stranger now that she's alone.

ACT I

One
Thorson's Funeral Chapel

October 15, 1918. In the Thorson funeral chapel in Unity, Saskatchewan, a fifteen year-old girl, SUNNA THORSON, applies makeup to the face of a corpse.

SUNNA: You never die, do you Uncle? People die, but you never do. Because how do you do that? Death is not being alive—and since being alive is what you know, experience, well how can you experience death? You can't. Because you aren't alive. So you never die. You can experience someone's death, you can know of his absence, but you, yourself, cannot die. So life is endless consciousness, right? While I'm alive, I'm the observer, I see things happen. When I die—well, I don't die, the perception just changes. I'm no longer the observer, but the observed. Someone might witness my death, but I never die.

Two
A Message

At the Unity Telegraph and Telephone office two women sit side by side at the plug board. The sound of an incoming telegraph message is heard. DORIS is recording the telegraph while eavesdropping on the conversation ROSE is having on the phone.

ROSE: Oh, my heart goes out to you, it really does.

DORIS: Mine too.

ROSE: Oh, yes ... both of ours ... yes, I know ...

DORIS: It's a trial.

ROSE: It's a trial, it really is. But she's in a better place now.

DORIS: But the poor baby.

ROSE: Is Mrs. Kuchinsky there?

DORIS: She's a dear soul.

ROSE: Good. Yes, she's a dear soul. Yes. She'll take care of the wee one, don't you worry. Well our prayers are with you Stan—

DORIS: And the poor baby.

ROSE: And the baby. A blessing really. A burden, but a blessing. A miracle. It's such a tragedy. Well, God bless.

> *She disconnects the line and immediately patches the cable into another trunk and rings.*

ROSE: I'll call the Thorson girl.

DORIS: You know Stan was lucky to find a wife.

ROSE: Yes, he was. I don't know what he'll do now. Hello Sunna.

DORIS: Strange girl.

ROSE: Yes, there's been some sad news. Ardell passed away last night.

DORIS: Poor thing.

ROSE: Yes, she was having her baby.

DORIS: How's he going to manage?

ROSE: No, no, it lived. Almost a shame, but it's a blessing really. Sad though, Dr. Lindsey was stuck up in Missing, just couldn't make it in time. And Mrs. Kuchinsky did what she could but ... No she was never very well was she?

DORIS: Sickly.

ROSE: Always seemed like something was wrong.

DORIS: And always that terrible smell. Shocks me they had any children.

ROSE: Oh, I suppose he'll bring her to you this morning. Will you manage?

DORIS: Imagine a girl ...

ROSE: Well, we'll all miss your uncle. He did his job well.

DORIS: Money-grubbing drunk is what he was.

ROSE: You know Sunna, Stan's not well off. Now with a child to look after, and he had a bad crop this year. I'm sure your uncle would have been sympathetic.

DORIS: Maybe Stan should marry that Thorson girl. Get out of farming. He'll need a wife.

ROSE: Well I'm sure you'll do right. I guess he'll want the funeral on Sunday. After the service for your uncle.

DORIS: It may be the only way she'd ever find a husband.

ROSE: Well, take care.

> DORIS *sighs as she reads the recently arrived telegraph message.*

ROSE: What does it say?

DORIS: Hand me a black ribboned envelope.

ROSE: Oh, no.

DORIS: Yes.

ROSE: Who?

DORIS: The Spooner boy.

ROSE: Rufus.

DORIS: He looked so proud the day he left in his uniform.

ROSE: Oh, his mother ...

DORIS: Remember how jealous he was, when the whole thing started, that he wasn't old enough to go with his brother?

ROSE: And now ...

18

DORIS: And now ... It's very cruel.

ROSE: France?

DORIS: Hmm?

ROSE: Did he die in France?

DORIS: No, in England.

ROSE: England?

DORIS: Yes, I don't think he even got to fight.

ROSE: What does it say?

DORIS: The usual, gave his life for the King and Country, honorably in service.

ROSE: Maybe it was pneumonia.

DORIS: That's true.

ROSE: It seems lots of the boys died of that in London, lately.

DORIS: That's true.

ROSE: Still so sad. I'll ring Millie.

DORIS. Well, wait 'til this is delivered.

ROSE: No, about Ardell.

DORIS: Oh, yes. So sad.

Three
Ardell

*Outside STAN's home. Offstage a baby is crying.
STAN enters dragging the body of Ardell wrapped in
a bloodstained sheet. He trips and falls backwards.*

STAN: Goddammit Ardell! Jesus.

He sits by the body for a while in silence.

STAN: Well ...

*Silence, then STAN cries softly for only a second, then
silence.*

STAN: What the hell ...

*He sighs and rests his head on the body's stomach.
Suddenly, a terrible farting noise emanates from the
corpse. STAN screams and recoils.*

STAN: Oh, Jesus! Ardell? Ardell?

*Long silence. Then a tortured, one syllable laugh
bursts from STAN.*

STAN: Even now ...

*STAN breaks down and sobs silently, curling up on
the ground away from the body. The baby cries in
the background. Lights fade.*

Four
A Dream

*In the darkness a match is struck and a lantern is
lit. BEATRICE surveys the night. Out of the blackness*

a very handsome teenaged boy appears, shirtless, as if just in from working outdoors. He holds a bundle of letters.

MICHAEL: Bea?

BEA: Glen?

MICHAEL: Happy birthday, Bea.

BEA: Glen?

MICHAEL: You waited.

> *The lantern is extinguished. The threshing machine roars.*

Five
The Preacher

Suddenly, it's daylight and BEATRICE is dismembering a chicken for dinner. In the distance MICHAEL is pitching stooks of wheat into the threshing machine off-stage.

BEA: October 16, 1918. Last night I dreamt Glen returned from the war. Only, in the dream, he didn't look like Glen—but I knew it was him and I could see in his eyes that he had missed me. In the dream he held love letters that I suppose I had written him. It was though he wanted me to read them; to remind me what I had said. It was as though he knew all along what I had been feeling. It was a silly dream really, but for some reason when I woke up I felt very nervous.

MICHAEL has stopped working and walked downstage. There's a sudden sound of a door slamming like a gunshot as he enters the kitchen. BEATRICE shrieks.

MICHAEL: Hello, Buzz!

BEA: Oh, you scared me Glen.

MICHAEL: What?

BEA: Don't sneak in like that.

MICHAEL: Who's Glen?

BEA: What?

MICHAEL: You just called me Glen.

BEA: No, I didn't.

MICHAEL: Yes you did. You said, "Oh, you scared me Glen." Who's Glen?

BEA: I said, "Michael."

MICHAEL: Nope. You're turning red, Buzz. I'd like to meet this fellow Glen, now.

BEA: I didn't. I said … Now what would you like? Aren't you freezing, like that?

MICHAEL: No, ma'am! The breeze is nice today. / I was working

BEA: It's freezing.

MICHAEL: up quite a sweat out there. I was hoping I might get some water, please.

BEA: Okay.

She pours him some water.

MICHAEL: Mmmm, chicken!

As he drinks she watches intently.

BEA: (*aside*) Michael was just fourteen when he came
to work on the Daniels' custom threshing crew
last year. He was big for his age, but filled his size
with the confidence of an Evangelist preacher.
And that became his name: "The Preacher."
Everything was glory, revelation, rapture. And
laughter. He was contagious. You caught Michael
just by being near him.

Back to normal.

MICHAEL: Hallelujah, that's good water!

SISSY runs in.

SISSY: Get to work preacher boy!

MICHAEL: Morning, Sizzle.

SISSY: Shirt caught in the thresher? / Again?

MICHAEL: No—I'll catch you in the thresher! No, I was
working up a pretty big sweat. Thought I'd save
my shirt the trouble of soakin' it up.

SISSY: Mighty thoughtful of ya! Now, could you do me a
favour or do you save them all for your shirt?

MICHAEL: Well, that shirt's been real good to me. What
have you ever done? Hey, Buzz?

BEA: I'm sure not much.

SISSY: I'm a girl.

MICHAEL: So?

SISSY: So it's your duty to be kind.

MICHAEL: My duty?

SISSY: Like goin' to war.

BEA: Sissy.

MICHAEL: Well, I'm not old enough to go to war.

SISSY: And if you were, would you go? Or would you be a slacker?

MICHAEL: I'm no slacker.

SISSY: Then reach up to the top shelf and get me that jar.

MICHAEL: Yes, sir!

> *As he raises his arms SISSY rushes him and tickles his armpits.*

MICHAEL: Hey!

SISSY: Where's your faithful shirt now?

MICHAEL: That's not very lady-like.

SISSY: I'm not old enough to be a lady.

MICHAEL: So do you want the jar or no?

SISSY: Oh, sure.

> *MICHAEL attempts to reach it and SISSY tickles him again.*

MICHAEL: Hey! For that, I'm not getting your jar.

SISSY: That's fine. I didn't really want it. Come with me!

She grabs his hand and takes him outside. BEATRICE picks up some yarn and knitting needles as she watches the two exit.

BEA: I watched Sissy and Michael walk into the field; noticed how far they could go and still be seen. Sissy pushing and poking Michael, their words floating out in the steam of their breath—I could see their conversation in clouds. How does she do it? Like it's easy to be near him—like her heart isn't cracking open and bleeding from within.

Six
A Prophecy

Outside.

MICHAEL: Ah! See this day? This is a good day!

SISSY: You're cold.

MICHAEL: Am not.

SISSY: You've got goosebumps.

MICHAEL: I love those things! That's just me trying to get out of my skin and get more of a day like this.

SISSY: You look like a featherless chicken boy. Ready for the oven.

MICHAEL: That makes me hungry. Look at my breath! It's like I'm smoking.

SISSY: Do you want to?

MICHAEL: Want to what?

SISSY: Smoke, chicken boy.

She takes out tobacco and paper.

MICHAEL: There's the old shirt! I've missed you buddy!

SISSY: Leave it off.

MICHAEL: Why? (*sees SISSY is rolling a cigarette*) Hey!

SISSY: You'll stop the day from gettin' in.

MICHAEL: You know, it's really freezing if you're not working. Where did you get that?

SISSY: My dad.

MICHAEL: How do you know how to do that?

SISSY: My dad.

MICHAEL: Your dad let's you smoke?

SISSY: Hey! He wouldn't be a very good dad if he let me smoke.

MICHAEL: Well you're not a very good daughter if you don't listen to your dad.

SISSY: My dad already has a good daughter. And there's a difference between what you're supposed to do and what you should do. / Here.

MICHAEL: Huh? What do you do?

SISSY: Just suck on it. It'll warm you up.

MICHAEL: That's not much of a fire. (*takes a drag*) Wow! Thank you! (*gives the cigarette back*)

SISSY: (*taking a drag*) You like it?

MICHAEL: No, it's absolutely terrible—Oh, a fire!

SISSY: What? (*she offers the cigarette again*)

MICHAEL: That's what we have to do. A big bonfire for Hallowe'en. (*waves off cigarette*) No thanks, I've figured that thing out all at once.

SISSY: I like a big fire too.

MICHAEL: Get some wood, chop it up.

SISSY: Better than that, start it in one of those haystacks. That could be a good fire.

MICHAEL: That's feed, though.

SISSY: You wanna know something?

MICHAEL: From you?

SISSY: Yeah, from me.

MICHAEL: What?

SISSY: I've been reading a book.

MICHAEL: (*picks up his shirt*) That is something.

SISSY: Silly. Don't put that shirt on, I told you.

MICHAEL: It's really cold!

SISSY: Don't! Listen. This book says that—you know in the Bible, at the end, there's the part about when the world ends? Everything is taken away.

MICHAEL: Yeah.

SISSY: This book says that it's going to happen this year.

MICHAEL: This year?

SISSY: This year!

MICHAEL: You're funnier than I thought.

27

SISSY: But it makes sense. The war. The weather. Strange things happening all around. Bad crops this year.

MICHAEL: Not so bad.

SISSY: Pretty bad though.

MICHAEL: Well, yeah, I guess.

SISSY: Listen. Okay, here. We know that the world has six thousand years. Start to finish. Do you believe that?

MICHAEL: I don't know.

SISSY: It's in the Bible.

MICHAEL: Okay, then.

SISSY: Now, also in the Bible, luckily, someone was smart enough to record how long everyone lived when the world was first made.

MICHAEL: And everyone's nine hundred years old or something.

SISSY: Yeah. Well when you count it all up and the time from then to when Jesus was born you get 4,082.

MICHAEL: Uh huh?

SISSY: So 4,082 years went by before Jesus was born. So if there's only 6,000 years in all, how many left after he was born? Until the end.

MICHAEL: I'm not so good at numbers.

SISSY: (*draws in the dirt*) 6,000 minus 4,082 equals 1,918. 1918. You've got goosebumps again.

MICHAEL: That's 'cause it's freezing.

SISSY: So, are you scared?

MICHAEL: Are you?

SISSY: No.

MICHAEL: How come?

SISSY: I don't know. But I'm not. I'm forming a special club. It allows both boys and girls. And it's the end of the world club.

MICHAEL: What do you get to do in the club?

SISSY: Anything you want.

MICHAEL: The end of the world doesn't scare you?

SISSY: Not if it's this year.

MICHAEL: Why not.

SISSY: Because it means you and I get to be the last people on earth!

She rubs his torso.

MICHAEL: What are you doing?

SISSY: Keeping you inside your skin for a little longer.

She kisses him then quickly stops.

SISSY: Put your shirt on preacher boy. People will think you're trying to impress me.

BEATRICE is watching them from the window. Frustrated and angry she knits at an insane rate. The needles clack together in a blur. Yarn is eaten up by the yard. The lights shift.

Seven
An Arrival

The sound transforms into the clicking of the telegraph. DORIS is reading a telegram that's just arrived.

DORIS: Oh my!

ROSE: What does it say?

DORIS: Next train.

> *DORIS gives her the telegram. ROSE takes one look and grabs a cable. She thinks for a second and then selects a trunk and patches it in.*

Eight
The War Effort

BEA is still knitting socks. A large pile rests beside her. SISSY bursts in singing.

BEA: You shouldn't waste Michael's time when there's so much to be done.

SISSY: Who says I'm wasting his time?

BEA: You'll get him sent back home. He's supposed to be working. Something you wouldn't know.

SISSY: There's more important things right now.

BEA: The end of the world?

SISSY: The end of the world.

BEA: Oh, well, if I were you, I'd try to straighten up a little for the big day. I don't think they'll let someone into heaven who can't do the washing.

SISSY: There's no washing in heaven.

BEA: That's because everyone there doesn't let it pile up all week.

SISSY: Maybe there's no heaven either.

BEA: Not for you.

SISSY: Well then yay for me if you're going to be there, annoying the whole afterlife with your depressing hobbies.

BEA: You know a woman can be a slacker too.

SISSY: Slacker?

BEA: Just because we can't fight doesn't mean we aren't part of the battle.

SISSY suddenly flies at BEATRICE and hits her.

BEA: Ow!

SISSY hits her again.

BEA: Ow! Sissy! Don't!

SISSY: I can fight. I could be that woman in the painting, / leading the

BEA: What painting?

SISSY: army, you know, where everybody's following her and she's carrying the flag over the hill, boobies hanging out of her dress and she doesn't even care.

BEA: Sissy!

SISSY: The enemy takes one look—"Gött in Himmel! I can see her boobies!"—and then it's, "arghh," right through the eye socket with the flagpole! / Keep your looks

BEA: Sissy!

SISSY: to yourself Fritz! (*pause*) I wish I *was* over there!

BEA: You're not right in the head.

SISSY: And you are? What are you doing to win the war? / Crochet?

BEA: Lot's. Yes! It's important. It helps.

SISSY: Helps you.

BEA: How? No.

SISSY: Helps you think you're doing something. Helps you forget. / Stops you

BEA: No.

SISSY: from thinking. / You're like

BEA: No.

SISSY: the ol' topper with the bottle. / Your brains are

BEA: I am not.

SISSY: softened by the click, click, click of your knitting needles. / Do you

BEA: No!

SISSY: think any boy over there wants to find your ugly socks in the mail? Look at the things! Makes me sad ... think about the poor boy opening his package in middle of a fight, "Oh, god, I hope it's not more ugly socks … / Oh … no! No! My country

BEA: He would not!

SISSY: hates me!" He'll turn the gun on himself right there!

BEA: You're wicked!

SISSY: And you're boring!

> *Silence.*

BEA: I'd rather be boring than … than …

SISSY: I know, and that's what's so horrible. (*tosses BEA a ball of yarn*) Have another drink! Toast the war.

> *The phone rings two short rings and then a long one.*

SISSY: Brambly's.

BEA: (*throws the yarn at the phone*) God! I want it to be over! I want it to be over! I can't think! I want things back to normal.

SISSY: This is normal now.

BEA: No!

> *The phone sounds with two short rings repeated. The girls look at each other.*

SISSY: Stone's!

> *When the phone stops ringing SISSY shoves a cloth into the mouthpiece and picks up the earpiece to listen.*

SISSY: There's a soldier on the next train. He's got a ticket for Unity.

BEA: Glen?

SISSY: (*shrugging her shoulders*) Let's go.

BEA: Ring Mary.

> *The phone suddenly sounds three short rings. SISSY answers.*

SISSY: Hello? We know! We're going now! Don't you hope so!

> *She hangs up.*

BEA: Mary?

SISSY: Let's go!

BEA: She thinks it's Richard?

SISSY: Richard, Richard, Richard! Glen, Glen, Glen!

> *They run off.*

Nine
The Train Station

> *Sound of a train arriving. Near the train station STAN pushes the body of Ardell in a wheelbarrow. It's slow going. The three girls arrive from the opposite direction from STAN. They're carrying makeshift bouquets made from wheat shafts. Everyone stops in an awkward silence. Suddenly, the train whistle blows. Everyone eagerly looks towards the platform and in the steam of the train a single soldier appears—he is blind (with his eyes*

34

*still bandaged) and decorated with the Victoria
Cross. Everyone stares.*

HART: Hello?

> *Silence.*

HART: Hello?

> *Silence. He takes a step forward and falls face-first
> off the platform. Everyone yells too late.*

STAN: Jesus!

MARY: Let me help you up.

> *The girls help him to his feet.*

SISSY: Are you all right?

HART: I'm fine, I'm fine. Thank you. Thank you.

> *Pause.*

STAN: You're in Unity son.

HART: Yes, they called it out on the train. It's not quite
as flat as I was told it would be.

STAN: Do you mean to be here?

HART: Sir?

STAN: I mean—

SISSY: He means who are you?

HART: My name's Hart. I've—

BEA: Is your family here?

HART: Yes. I mean—well, I've come to see my father.
Hjortur Thorson. At the funeral home.

MARY: Oh.

SISSY: Ah, uh—

BEA: Your father?

STAN: Ah, well. I see. I'm on my way there myself son.
I'll take you.

HART: Oh, you are? Are you …

STAN: My wife passed on yesterday.

HART: I'm sorry.

STAN: Well, let's go then.

MARY: Um, I guess these are for you.

> *She hands him a bouquet.*

HART: What's that? A broom?

MARY: It's a bouquet.

> *He smells it.*

HART: Um … Thank you.

STAN: Probably best if you just put one hand on my
shoulder and follow me.

> *There is a strange procession. STAN pushing Ardell
> in the wheelbarrow, the blind soldier following with
> one hand on STAN's shoulder to guide him, the three
> girls with their wheat bouquets. From a distance a
> haunting Ukrainian funeral song is heard.*

SISSY: I'm Sissy!

HART: Oh, hi.

MARY: And Mary.

HART: Hello.

BEA: Beatrice.

HART: Hello there.

SISSY: And me, Sissy!

BEA: You said.

SISSY: Hi!

HART: Hi. Pleased to meet you.

MARY: And that's Stan you're holding on to.

HART: Of course. Thank you sir.

STAN: Well are we all going then? Come on.

HART: I guess you might have been hoping I'd be
    someone else.

SISSY: Mary's boyfriend is in the war.

MARY: Sissy's boyfriend's too young to fight.

SISSY: I don't have a / boyfriend.

HART: You got your man overseas?

MARY: His name's Richard Stone. Do you know him?

HART: I'm sorry, I don't think so.

BEA: (*aside*) A soldier. A wounded soldier. So beautiful,
    so horribly beautiful. And we all wanted from
    him something we had been waiting so long
    for—contact with that other world. A story. A war
    story. But instead he just talked about how every-
    one in Halifax had the flu.

SISSY: Ew.

HART: Well it's bad.

MARY: I'm lucky I don't get sick.

HART: People are dying.

SISSY: From the flu?

HART: A lot of people.

SISSY: I had the flu already this spring. I kind of liked it. / Lying around a lot.

HART: Not like this.

BEA: Seems strange.

HART: Young people mostly.

SISSY: Dying?

HART: Yep.

SISSY: Wow. Plague. Plague's a sign.

BEA: Shhh!

MARY: What are they going to do?

HART: Well, what are you going to do? It's coming this way.

SISSY: The flu is coming?

HART: On the train in Montreal I heard people there were starting to get it. Toronto too.

STAN: Well, that's the good thing about living out here. You can see things coming from a long ways off.

> *Suddenly STAN accidentally upsets the wheelbarrow and Ardell's body tumbles out. There is a shocked silence. The soldier is unaware of what has happened.*

HART: Drop something?

STAN: Just hold up a minute there.

> *STAN attempts to load the corpse back in the wheel-barrow. BEATRICE tries to help, but he waves her away.*

STAN: Get away! Jesus.

> *BEATRICE retreats. Eventually he succeeds and they carry on.*

STAN: Well, I don't think we all need to be going there like some sort of parade. Why don't you girls go home? I'm sure you've got things to do.

> *STAN exits with the soldier trailing behind.*

SISSY: It's a plague.

BEA: What?

SISSY: The flu is a plague.

MARY: Sounds like it.

SISSY: It's one of the four horsemen of the apocalypse.

BEA: Sissy, stop it.

SISSY: It's really coming.

MARY: Poor Ardell.

BEA: And poor Stan.

SISSY: The soldier didn't even know!

MARY: Sissy, that's mean!

SISSY: What's mean? Nobody did anything on purpose. But there he was. "Drop something?"

MARY: Sissy!

SISSY: "Uh, just my wife."

BEA: Sissy, you're wretched.

SISSY: I'm sorry. I've never seen anything like that. I mean I was kind of glad for him, that he couldn't see. But us—(*gasps*) Ardell is Sunna's first customer!

MARY: I really can't imagine.

SISSY: Let's go spy.

BEA: Spy?

SISSY: Come on. We've got to figure out who this soldier is.

MARY: There's no windows.

SISSY: Well, we could just bring over the rest of the bouquets.

BEA: He thought it was a broom.

SISSY: He liked it.

MARY: There's no smell.

SISSY: Come on you two!

BEA: No. Maybe later. Let them be for a bit. Respect.

SISSY: I'm just so curious what they do in there. What happens inside?

BEA: I don't know.

MARY: I don't want to.

The mortuary is created as SISSY imagines.

SISSY: There's probably a big table where they put you. And a big bucket for your guts. And a bunch of knives and hooks and / needles and thread

MARY: Hooks?

SISSY: for sewing you up. And a pile of hay to stuff you with.

BEA: They don't stuff you.

SISSY: Nowadays that's what they do.

MARY: Let's go. It's cold.

SISSY: One day we should go though. See what's there.

Ten
Family

In the mortuary. SUNNA greets STAN as he arrives.

SUNNA: Hello.

STAN: (*he shakes her hand lamely*) Well ... So, uh here she is. She's got a bit of dirt here, uh ... I uh ... I couldn't ...

> *SUNNA takes the sheet off and examines the corpse. She grabs an arm and squeezes the flesh and moves it around. She then pushes on the body's stomach. Another loud fart. STAN looks away from all this.*

SUNNA: Hmm. That's smelly. What time was it when she died?

STAN: I don't know.

> *SUNNA notices HART standing in the doorway.*

SUNNA: Who's he?

STAN: Oh, your cousin is here. Come in son.

SUNNA: Cousin?

HART: Who's that?

STAN: It's your cousin.

HART: My cousin?

STAN: Yes, it's ... well tell him your name girl.

SUNNA: Sunna Gudmundsdóttir.

HART: From Iceland?

SUNNA: Who are you?

HART: I'm Hart. Uh, Hjortur is my father. He didn't tell you?

SUNNA: No.

HART: I live in Halifax. Or I used to. With my mother. Before ...

SUNNA: Oh. What's wrong with your eyes?

HART: They're burnt.

STAN: Um, do you want me to move her somewhere?

SUNNA: No. Leave her.

HART: Is my father here?

SUNNA: Yes, over here. (*to STAN*) Excuse me.

> *SUNNA guides HART to the coffin. He is confused for a moment.*

HART: Father?

He touches the body and his hand accidentally finds his father's face.

HART: Ah. Oh. I see. When … When did this happen?

SUNNA: You didn't know? Why are you here?

STAN: Well, I'll … I'll be back later, Sunna. To settle up.

SUNNA: It's fifteen for burial.

STAN: Right. Good. Thank you. Well, uh, good-bye.

> *He suddenly gives her a desperate, awkward hug, which lasts several seconds. SUNNA neither resists nor participates. STAN quickly leaves. SUNNA notices HART is still feeling his father's face.*

HART: He feels greasy.

SUNNA: You're messing up the colouring.

HART: Sorry. I'm trying to remember what he looks like.

SUNNA: Oh.

HART: I think the last time I saw him I was four. He brought a body with him?

SUNNA: Huh?

HART: Stan brought a body with him?

SUNNA: His wife.

HART: How did she die?

SUNNA: Had a baby. She wasn't very strong.

HART: And what are you doing?

43

SUNNA: Get her ready for the funeral.

HART: So you've taken over? (*pause*) So, we're cousins? Where are your parents?

SUNNA: I don't know. I don't remember them.

HART: Are you an orphan?

SUNNA: They sent me here a long time ago.

HART: Oh, how come?

SUNNA: Too many children.

HART: Funny I never heard about that. Father never wrote much. Sent some money every now and then. Not much else.

HART: How old are you?

SUNNA: (*snaps*) Forty. Why are you asking me all these questions?

HART: I don't know what else to do.

    Pause.

SUNNA: Do you want to stay here?

HART: Here?

SUNNA: The house part is in the back. There's a cot you can use.

HART: Thanks.

SUNNA: Do you speak Icelandic?

HART: No. My mother was English.

SUNNA: Oh.

HART: What are you doing? What's that noise?

SUNNA: I'm draining out the blood. Putting in the preserve.

HART: Preserve?

SUNNA: Embalming fluid. Keeps the body from rotting.

HART: You do that here?

SUNNA: Yes.

HART: I would have imagined you would just dig a hole and that would be it.

SUNNA: Well people are getting used to this. Now there's more time to prepare a funeral. You don't have to worry about the person stinking up the church.

HART: And do you take care of everything?

SUNNA: That's the job. People don't want to have to concern themselves with all of this. Graveyard, funeral, casket ... lots to think about.

HART: Sure. My dad taught you how to do it?

SUNNA: I just watched. I don't think he expected me to do it after him. I don't think he thought about those things.

HART: Lots of surprises these days.

SUNNA: Yeah.

> *The scene fades. Outside the mortuary* BEATRICE *is revealed.*

BEA: October 16, 1918. P.S. For some time now I've had the awful sense of being spread around the world. My thoughts and feelings stretched across the ocean. It's terribly distracting and not the least bit comfortable. We—I have been waiting for it all to come back home again. To feel whole once more and able to think. Today, on the train, the world started to return. But not like I thought.

The lights fade away.

Eleven
In Need

A new day. The Stone residence. MARY answers the telephone. STAN appears.

MARY: Hello?

STAN: Mary? It's Stan.

MARY: Oh, hello Stan.

STAN: I was hoping I'd find you there. How's Mrs. Stone doing?

MARY: She's sleeping. Um … I'm very sorry about Ardell, Stan.

STAN: I, uh … Oh, geez …

MARY: It must be very hard.

STAN: Well, I'm sure she's in a better place.

MARY: Yes, I'm sure.

BEATRICE enters MARY's area. She brings a newspaper and her journal. MARY motions her to sit so she begins to write as she listens in on MARY's conversation.

STAN: I'm just having a little trouble getting everything done before winter.

MARY: Uh huh.

STAN: The baby ...

MARY: Yes.

STAN: Wasn't much of a harvest.

MARY: No.

STAN: And the weather.

MARY: It must be hard right now.

STAN: And then this flu.

MARY: Doesn't it sound horrible.

BEA: October 20, 1918. Word of the flu is spreading quickly. Like the flu itself. I wonder if ideas are contagious like that? If they float on the wind travelling from person to person infecting the brain.

STAN: There seems to be no end to the troubles.

MARY: No. It's frightening, all this.

STAN: Don't want my child to get sick for lack of attention.

MARY: I've been praying.

STAN: Don't know anymore.

MARY: I've been praying for all of us. For you.

BEA: (*whispering*) Who's that?

MARY: (*mouthing the word*) Stan.

STAN: It's hard.

MARY: Yes.

STAN: Oh, it is. I need someone ... I need someone to help with the baby. And the house. Mary would you like to ... Would you be able to come give me hand? Come live here. 'Til maybe things get a little better. Or even ...

MARY: Well, I'm looking after Richard's mother, uh, Mrs. Stone.

STAN: Oh, I know. You're a real help to her. But I was thinking ...

MARY: Richard will be home soon.

STAN: Sure. And then things would be easier for his mother. Maybe then you could ...

MARY: And we're getting married.

STAN: Pardon?

MARY: When Richard comes home we're getting married.

STAN: Oh.

MARY: I could try to maybe—

STAN: I called on the Wilde girls.

MARY: Oh yeah?

STAN: But they're pretty tied to their farm. That young one says.

MARY: Yes. I'm sorry.

STAN: Don't know what's the matter with girls these days.

MARY: Well …

STAN: These might be our last days on earth. You'd think people would be thinking of that …

MARY: Uh …

STAN: Well I best get back to the field.

MARY: I'm sorry Stan.

STAN: Some threatening clouds up there.

MARY: I—

He hangs up. Lights out on STAN.

MARY: Poor Stan.

BEA: He's not doing very well.

MARY: No.

BEA: The flu hit Regina yesterday.

MARY: It did? Oh, Bea, I'm scared.

BEA: (*aside*) October 20, 1918, P.S. Everyone's scared.

MARY: I wish Richard was home.

BEA: (*reading from newspaper*) Listen to this: More Tales of Canadian Bravery. A captain of a mounted rifle battalion, when his men were being decimated by machine gun fire, although wounded in the head and gassed, dashed forward alone into an enemy machine gun nest and armed only with rifle and bayonet, killed four and took eight prisoners. His magnificent bravery turned imminent defeat into victory.

MARY: Beatrice, I'm so scared. What if the flu comes here? And we get it. I get it ... and die. / And then Richard

BEA: Oh, Mary.

MARY: comes home ... only then he ... and I'm not here. And he ... gets off the train and he's in his uniform and he's expecting to see me ... and ... and ... then he finds out ... Oh, I can't stand it!

She cries.

BEA: (*to diary*) Most people don't want to die because they don't want to die. Mary doesn't want to die because it will make someone else feel bad. (*to MARY*) Well, we just have to be brave like a soldier.

MARY: (*cheering up*) Let's kiss his picture for good luck.

BEA: (*aside*) Mrs. Stone had a photograph taken of Richard before he left to fight. In the picture he held one end of the Union Jack.

MARY: Here.

MARY kisses the picture.

BEA: (*aside*) The other end was held by Glen.

MARY: Kiss Richard for good luck.

BEA: I feel silly.

MARY: Kiss him!

BEATRICE takes the picture and looks at it for a moment, looks at MARY, smiles. Long kiss. Bells ring, scene shifts.

Twelve
Contagion

DORIS is on the phone. There's a ring and ROSE patches a cable into one of the trunks.

DORIS: Yes the flu is a "reportable" disease.

ROSE: Central.

DORIS: It means you have to report / occurrences of

ROSE: Hello, Mr. McNulty.

DORIS: it to the health authorities.

ROSE: Hmm?

DORIS: Well, because people are dying front and rear.

ROSE: Well, yes you heard right then, no spitting. / Not in public.

DORIS: If you have it they put a notice on your door. You're quarantined.

ROSE: I know, but it's a twenty-five dollar fine. That's right twenty-five / dollars.

DORIS: Well no, you wouldn't go into the home of someone with a notice on their door.

ROSE: I didn't make it up.

DORIS: Mmm-hmmm.

ROSE: Mmm-hmmm.

DORIS: Mmm-hmmm.

ROSE: Well, you'll just have to keep it in your mouth / won't you?

DORIS: Well you'd report it because it's the law. (*to ROSE*) She wants to know why you'd report the flu in your house if it means that suddenly everyone avoids you like you have the plague.

ROSE: (*to DORIS*) It's not like the plague it is the plague! / (back into phone) Mr. McNulty, I think

DORIS: Mernie, you … what's that?

ROSE: it's perfectly "natural" not to spit. / Personally, I never spit.

DORIS: Of course you can report someone else. I think it's your duty if they're not behaving / responsible.

ROSE: Well, not being a man, I guess I wouldn't know about anything about "saliva build-up." Why don't you just swallow? Besides, spitting won't be a very good idea if you're wearing a mask, will it?

DORIS: You don't have the flu do you?

ROSE: Mask. That's also / the law.

DORIS: Well, and you won't if you avoid people's homes who have the notice on their door.

ROSE: You can buy them or make them, but you can't go out without one.

DORIS: (*to ROSE*) She wants to know if wc'd still come by if she had a notice on her door.

ROSE: (*to DORIS*) No. Of course not.

DORIS: (*back to phone*) Of course we would. No we wouldn't / forget about you.

ROSE: (*back to phone*) What's that? Oh, no I'm not wearing a mask. Because, I'm just here with Doris and she's not sick.

DORIS: Well take care then, I'll talk to you soon. Be careful. (*she disconnects*) I'm not sick!

A telegraph comes in and DORIS records it.

ROSE: It doesn't ... No, you can't catch the flu over the phone.

DORIS: What?

ROSE: How do I know? I just know, that's all. It's common sense. Can you smell my breath? (*she breathes heavily into the phone*)

DORIS: Who is that?

ROSE: Feel this wind? (*blows noisily into the mouthpiece*)

DORIS: Is that Gerald?

ROSE: No, you did not! No you didn't! There's no germs through the phone lines. / But you should

DORIS: Such a fool.

ROSE: wear a mask if you're going out threshing. Outdoors is exactly where it'll get you, and kill you right where you stand without a drop of mercy. Yes. Okay then. Yes. God bless you too. (*violently disconnects*) He's a complete idiot!

ROSE notices that DORIS is putting on a mask.

ROSE: What are you doing?

DORIS tosses a mask to ROSE and reads from the telegraph.

DORIS: It's a message for the doctor. Three more dead in Rosetown.

ROSE goes to the door and checks outside.

ROSE: The wind is blowing in from the east.

She returns and grabs the mask. Scene shifts.

Thirteen
Another Dream

In the darkness a match is struck and a lantern is lit. BEA carries flowers and wears a veil. A coffin rests on the stage with a body laid out. BEA approaches the body.

BEA: I love you Glen.

BODY: I love you Beatrice.

BEA: I waited for you.

BODY: I knew that you would.

BEA: Did you get my socks?

BODY: They were lovely. They helped me win the war.

BEA: They did? I knitted them special.

BODY: Come closer.

BEA: I'm not supposed to.

BODY: It's okay. Come closer.

BEA: Glen?

BODY: Come inside. With me.

BEA: Oh, Glen.

> *BEATRICE moves towards the coffin. Suddenly SISSY pops out.*

SISSY: You can't come in here, Beatrice. This is a two person coffin only.

BEA: Sissy!

SISSY: You have to find your own.

BEA: You ruin everything!

SISSY: You don't even know how to die.

BEA: I do. I do so. Glen? Glen!

> *The coffin shuts and BEATRICE is alone. Darkness.*

Fourteen
Over There

> *BEATRICE sits nervously with paper and ink. After a moment, she begins a letter.*

Bea: Dear Glen,
This is Beatrice Wilde writing to you. Remember me? I'm writing to let you know how proud Unity is of you.
Well, I'm also writing to say that if I were in charge I'd say that you've done your share and that you should come home. Because now it's

here where people are wounded in the heart and mind, and need you to help them win their peace back.

I can't even imagine what you must think of day to day. I suppose it's life and death and trying to be brave. But if you ever find yourself wondering if any of it's worth anything at all (because lately I find myself wondering about all manner of things I thought I knew to be true), then you can know: it is.

And if I can replace one hard thought with one thought that's not so hard, of someone far from you, but close, who prays you're well, and for your fast return, then perhaps that is all this letter is meant to do.

So now I send you a little memory from home. Today I saw the horses gathered in the basin outside of town. You know how you'll always find them licking the salt that appears on the surface of the earth there? I think they do that to increase their thirst for water ... to feel the need to drink in life.

    Pause.

I hold a memory of you, just before you left for war. Every day I run it over the edges of my heart—to increase my thirst for your return. With admiration, and perhaps some love, Bea ... atrice

> *Suddenly, she is outside the mortuary. She paces, holding the letter to Glen in her hand. Finally she knocks*

HART: Hello?

BEA: Hello?

HART: Who's there?

BEA: Is that …

HART: Who is that?

BEA: Beatrice Wilde.

HART: From the train station?

BEA: That's right.

HART: Come in.

BEA: (*opens door*) Hello?

HART: Come in.

> BEA *enters the mortuary. The soldier sits alone in*
> *the dark. He's not wearing shoes or socks. There is a*
> *dripping sound in the background.*

BEA: Are you by yourself here?

HART: Are you looking for Sunna?

BEA: No. / I wanted—

HART: Oh. Apparently my father's dead.

BEA: Yes.

HART: If you were looking for him.

BEA: No. I'm sorry. / I was just—

HART: It's okay. I think he's out in the ice shed—'til
the funeral.

BEA: Oh … Is Ardell in the ice shed?

HART: Is that uh, Mr. uh, Stan's wife?

BEA: Yes.

HART: Yep, she's out there too. You can go and see her if you want. / I think.

BEA: No. I ... uh ... not now.

HART: What brings you around? I hope everything's okay.

BEA: Oh, it is. I just thought I'd check and see how things were for you.

HART: Oh, I'm very well, thank you.

BEA: You are?

HART: Oh sure.

BEA: I'm sorry about your father.

HART: It's okay, but I was a bit surprised.

BEA: You didn't know?

HART: No.

BEA: Oh, dear.

HART: Kind of a cold reception.

BEA: Oh.

HART: Oh well.

BEA: Where's your mother now?

HART: She's dead too.

BEA: No.

HART: Flu.

BEA: No!

HART: Brother too.

BEA: Oh, no!

HART: Yep.

BEA: Flu?

HART: No, no, he got blown up last year when the city exploded. Did you want to come in and sit down?

BEA: I don't know that I should. I just— Where did your cousin go?

HART: She went out somewhere or something.

BEA: Oh. I've never actually been in here before. I'm not sure I'm allowed.

HART: Oh, I doubt Sunna would mind. You can keep me company for a bit.

BEA: How come it's so dark?

HART: Is it?

BEA: Oh, I'm sorry.

HART: Why? No, I just didn't know. Is there a lantern?

BEA: Yes, but it's not lit.

HART: You can light it.

BEATRICE lights the lantern.

BEA: You have a medal.

HART: Huh? Oh, yeah. They were just tossing these things out like jelly drops at a parade. / No school today?

BEA: I'm certain they weren't. Sorry, what?

HART: Sorry.

BEA: No, you were saying?

HART: Oh, I asked if there was no school today. Do you have the day free?

BEA: Oh, there's no free days right now. The harvest was late this year. They're still threshing.

HART: Oh, right. From school though.

BEA: I don't go to school.

HART: Oh, you're finished?

BEA: Yes, a while back.

HART: How old are you?

BEA: Ninet—uh, I mean I just turned twenty. One.

HART: Oh. You sound a little younger.

BEA: I do?

HART: Sorry. No. I mean, not much younger. Just ...

BEA: It's okay.

Silence. Then suddenly they speak in unison.

HART: / So, what's threshing?

BEA: So how long were—sorry, what?

HART: No, you were saying?

BEA: No, I'm sorry I interrupted.

HART: Oh, I just asked, what's threshing?

BEA: Oh. It's uh ... separating the wheat from the chaff.

HART: How do you do that?

BEA: With machines?

HART: Oh yeah.

> *Silence.*

HART: Sunna should be back soon.

BEA: Oh, I suppose I should go then.

HART: Should you?

BEA: Should I?

HART: No.

BEA: Oh.

> *Silence.*

BEA: So how long were you overseas?

HART: I went right at the beginning.

BEA: You did?

HART: Yep.

BEA: How was it?

HART: Oh, it was good enough. 'Cept my feet were always wet and got a little rotten. See them?

BEA: Oh, yeah.

HART: They're awful itchy all the time. What's that noise?

BEA: What noise.

HART: It's like dripping. Do you hear it?

BEA: No.

Silence, soft dripping.

BEA: No. I don't think so.

HART: Hmm.

BEA: Did you get packages?

HART: Hmm?

BEA: Did you get packages, or letters while you were over there?

HART: Sure. My mother wrote.

BEA: Did you get parcels?

HART: From her?

BEA: Well, no. I mean, I've been knitting socks for the men fighting over there and then they get sent away. Did you ever get socks?

HART: Socks?

BEA: Or things.

HART: No, no socks. Except the army socks. You got one pair until they disintegrated. Then you could apply for another pair.

BEA: That doesn't sound very nice.

HART: Not so bad.

BEA: Did your mother have to know where you were to write to you?

HART: Know where I was? No, I didn't even know where I was most of the time. And you couldn't say if you did. The censors would cut it out with a razor blade.

BEA: Must be hard to have other people read your letters.

HART: Well, I didn't have anything too personal to say.

BEA: So if I wanted to write to a soldier, how would I make sure he got it?

HART: Well, I doubt you could ever be sure that he got it until he writes you back.

BEA: But how would I address it?

HART: Do you know what division he's in?

BEA: No.

HART: But he's in the army.

BEA: Yes.

HART: Not the navy?

BEA: Oh. I don't know. I don't think so.

HART: Hmm. Might be hard. But you could always give it a go. See what happens.

BEA: Just his name on an envelope?

HART: "Canadian Army" "Overseas" maybe. See what happens. Is he someone special?

BEA: Just a friend from town.

HART: Well then, ask his family what division he's in.

BEA: I guess I could do that.

HART: Sure, why not?

BEA: I'm just not very …

HART: Hmm?

BEA: No, I guess I could do that.

> *The door bursts open with a bang and* SUNNA *enters carrying a body wrapped in a blanket over her shoulder. She drops it onto the table.*

HART: Is that you Sunna?

SUNNA: Yes.

HART: I'm just talking with uh … Beatrice here.

SUNNA: I see.

HART: So where were you off to.

SUNNA: Dent farm.

HART: Oh, did you bring somebody home?

SUNNA: Yes.

HART: Oh that's too bad. What happened?

SUNNA: Fell in front of the mower. / Don't know how

BEA: Oh my God!

SUNNA: he did it.

HART: And it killed him?

SUNNA: Yes.*

HART: Shame.

BEA: *Oh my God! Who?

SUNNA: Alfred Spooner.

BEA: Oh no!

HART: Did you know him, Beatrice?

BEA: Oh, oh no! He's their last boy.

SUNNA: I know that. I've got to fix him up so his mother can look at him.

> *SUNNA takes off a makeshift satchel slung around her shoulder and puts it on the table next to the body.*

BEA: What's in there?

SUNNA: That's his head.

> *Horrified silence. Then BEATRICE turns and exits the mortuary.*

HART: I wish I could be of some help.

SUNNA: It's fine. What have you been doing?

HART: Listened to the phone for a while. Lot's of people talking about the flu. Where do the coffins come from?

SUNNA: We build them in the shed. Wood comes in from Saskatoon.

HART: Maybe I could help put them together. You might need a lot soon.

SUNNA: You know, I think the flu is being spread by soldiers coming home.

HART: Yeah? (*pause*) You're probably right. (*pause*) I don't have the flu.

SUNNA: I know.

HART: But people might think …

SUNNA: People need excuses.

HART: But there's no flu here yet.

SUNNA: No. Do you think that will last?

HART: No. (*pause*) Should I go?

SUNNA: Where?

HART: Away.

SUNNA: Halifax?

HART: You know, I don't really have anyone in Halifax either. I was away so long.

SUNNA: Were you thinking of staying here?

HART: I don't know. I don't suppose I'm much use.

SUNNA: In the shed there's lumber. There's a hammer and nails and a saw. There's three coffins too. Go and try to build one. One try only though. I can't have wood wasted. There won't be any more coming for a while.

HART: Okay. Thank you. And are you okay?

SUNNA: Okay?

HART: With … With doing that.

SUNNA: I like working.

HART: Okay. You didn't know him?

SUNNA: No more than anybody else.

HART: Okay. Is this the door?

SUNNA: That's the cupboard. Left. No, left.

>   *HART finds the door.*

SUNNA: One try only, remember.

>   *HART exits.*

Fifteen
A Letter

*MARY is working at Richard's mom's house.
There's a knock at the door. MARY opens it and
MICHAEL is there. He wears a mask.*

MARY: Yes?

MICHAEL: Is Mrs. Stone up?

MARY: No, she's resting, what is it? What's wrong?

> *MICHAEL holds a telegram with a black border. He
> holds it out towards MARY. MARY sees it and
> recoils.*

MICHAEL: Uh, I'm sorry …

> *A pause. A series of strange gestures as she tries to
> erase the moment, then she pushes past MICHAEL
> and runs off as BEATRICE enters. MICHAEL has exit-
> ed into the house.*

BEA: Mary? October 22, 1918. Overheard some people
talking about the soldier, Hart. They thought it
was a bad idea that a man that had been around
the flu out east was now in town, and that it was
lucky for us he couldn't move around too much.
I wanted to say, "He's a hero." I wanted to tell
them about his medal; tell them that the fact he
was badly wounded indeed made them lucky but
for a very different reason. But it would be no
use with these types. Also, yesterday they tore
down the new Spooner barn, which was only half
done. Heard they couldn't afford to finish it.

> *She walks into the street. SUNNA appears carrying
> an impossibly large load of wood on one shoulder*

and a hammer in the opposite hand. SUNNA drops the hammer and not wanting to set the load down attempts to get it with her foot. BEA watches her struggle for a minute.

BEA: Spooner barn? (*pause*) That must be heavy.

SUNNA: Can you get that hammer?

BEA: Oh, okay. Sorry.

> *BEA picks up the hammer and hands it to SUNNA.*

BEA: What's it for?

SUNNA: Coffins.

BEA: Oh no. Who died?

SUNNA: I don't know. We'll see.

> *In the telegraph office ROSE and DORIS are wearing masks, camphor sacks around their necks, and are brewing a foul smelling concoction on the wood stove. MARY runs up and knocks at the door.*

ROSE: Who's there?

MARY: It's Mary, let me in!

ROSE: (*peeking out*) Where's your mask?

MARY: Let me in! It's Richard!

DORIS: Give her some—

ROSE: Drink this first.

MARY: What?

ROSE: Drink it.

DORIS: It'll kill germs.

ROSE: It kills germs. Drink it.

MARY: Ow! It's hot.

DORIS: She's got to drink it fast.

ROSE: Don't sip it girl. Drink it down!

MARY: Ow, it's burning!

DORIS: It's no good if it cools.

ROSE: Is it cooling?

MARY: No. My mouth is burnt—I'm not sick. Please let me in.

DORIS: Give her the mask.

ROSE: Put this on.

> *MARY puts on the mask and is allowed in.*

DORIS: What is it?

ROSE: Why the panic?

MARY: It's Richard.

ROSE: Oh, dove.

MARY: It's a mistake.

DORIS: I'm sorry sweet.

MARY: It's someone else.

DORIS: Love.

MARY: Another Richard.

ROSE: No. Sit. It's terrible, but we must be thankful.

MARY: For what?

ROSE: He was a hero.

DORIS: Oh.

MARY: What?

DORIS: The mail came in on the train this morning. I saw there was a letter from Richard.

MARY: Richard.

DORIS: Addressed to you.

MARY: Oh, give it!

DORIS reaches towards a stack of mail.

ROSE: No! Don't touch it!

DORIS stops.

MARY: Richard!

ROSE: Those letters carry germs. I'm sorry, but Richard had … it. He died from … it.

MARY: I don't care.

ROSE: Have you ever seen—I've seen drawings of them in the newspaper—they're too small to see, but with a telescope they peer right down. And a more hideous creature you never saw.

DORIS: What are you on about?

ROSE: The germs. A thousand little teeth and they eat you from within.

DORIS: We'll just bake the letter for a bit to kill those nasty buggers. Give me the letter and I'll put it in the oven for a spell.

MARY: How long?

DORIS: How long would it take to kill those germs?

ROSE: Use the egg timer.

> ROSE *produces a wind-up egg timer.*

MARY: Hurry!

ROSE: Dove, the letter's not going anywhere.

MARY: I need to read it now!

DORIS: Mary, put the letter in the oven.

> MARY *carefully picks up the letter and puts it in the oven and* ROSE *winds the timer. The three watch intently into the open oven staring at the letter as the timer ticks. An eternity passes.*

MARY: (*whispers*) That's enough.

DORIS: Shh!

> *The bell suddenly rings and the letter bursts into flames.*

MARY: Richard!

DORIS: Oh, lord!

> *They reach for the burning envelope.* DORIS *burns her wrist on the stove and screams. The pull their arms out.* MARY *reaches back and pulls the letter out and they try to extinguish the flames but there are only ashes by the end. The telegraph office dissolves.*

MARY: (*holding ashes*) Richard.

Sixteen
Fear

*BEATRICE alone. As she records her thoughts the cast
assembles with her on stage.*

BEA: October 25, 1918. The town has been
quarantined. Not because of illness, but because
of fear of illness. No one is allowed to enter or
leave. Well, you can leave, but you won't get back
in. Trains have been ordered not to stop. No pick
ups or deliveries. The mail is piled outside of
town and will be burned later.

BEA, ROSE, DORIS: Unity will not be victim to this
disease.

BEA: Hallowe'en is cancelled.

SISSY: Schools are closed.

STAN: No spitting, hacking, coughing or clearing
throats to speak.

MICHAEL: No kissing.

DORIS: No public gatherings.

ROSE: No church.

MARY: No weddings.

BEA: No funerals.

SUNNA: Only quick and tidy burials.

BEA: We hear the news daily of towns decimated by the
disease. So many deaths. So many sick and
unable to work. But we know that it is only a
matter of conviction.

BEA, DORIS, STAN: Know the enemy.

BEA: The mistake made is that people think it can't be helped.

STAN and SUNNA: That it is invisible and unstoppable.

MICHAEL: But we know otherwise.

SISSY: The flu is only alive when it is inside us.

SISSY and MICHAEL: That is how it survives.

MARY: So it's true that the enemy is invisible.

ROSE and DORIS: But don't look for the enemy.

SUNNA and SISSY: Look for the horse he rides.

STAN: And then you see him coming.

ALL: The enemy is you.

BEA: The enemy is me.

Seventeen
Hallowe'en

MICHAEL and SISSY are walking at night.

MICHAEL: Look at that moon!

SISSY: Listen.

MICHAEL: Yeah.

SISSY: Hear it?

MICHAEL: Yeah.

SISSY: Silence.

MICHAEL: Yeah.

SISSY: It's all ours. Empty world and everything is ours.

MICHAEL: Yeah. Too bad they cancelled Hallowe'en—
it's my favorite.

SISSY: Me too.

MICHAEL: Do you like being scared?

SISSY: Yeah. Do you?

MICHAEL: Yeah. Everything changes in the dark. Feels
like things are watching you. Look at those
bushes. Something might be hiding in there
right now watching us, listening to us, and there's
nothing that can help us.

He suddenly roars in an attempt to frighten SISSY.

SISSY: Let's be that thing.

MICHAEL: What?

SISSY: Let's be the monster in the bush.

MICHAEL: How?

SISSY: Let's you and I crawl into that bush and watch.
Wait for some poor person to come along the
road—let's be the thing they're scared of.

MICHAEL: Go on!

SISSY: I mean it. Let's do it.

MICHAEL: I'm not crawling in that bush!

SISSY: Why not?

MICHAEL: Because ... because, what if there is
something in there.

SISSY: Do you think there is?

MICHAEL: I don't know ... it's dark ... anything can happen.

SISSY: Let's be that thing.

MICHAEL: Yeah? And what if there's something already being that thing?

SISSY: Then we'll be eaten alive! Come on chicken boy.

They begin to crawl into the bushes.

MICHAEL: This is really scary!

SISSY: I know!

MICHAEL: It's great!

SISSY: I know. Here. Now we're the thing.

MICHAEL: So it's true. There are things hiding in the bushes and waiting to get you.

SISSY: Yep.

MICHAEL: We should do this tomorrow night.

SISSY: For Hallowe'en?

MICHAEL: Yeah.

SISSY: Okay. We should have the fire too.

MICHAEL: But they won't let anybody come.

SISSY: It's okay. Just for us.

MICHAEL: A bonfire for two people?

SISSY: The biggest one ever!

MICHAEL: Okay. (*pause*) I hope someone comes along.

Sissy: Yeah.

> *They watch. In the distance the haunting Ukrainian funeral song is heard. MARY passes by alone dressed in mourning. Then STAN passes by pushing his empty wheelbarrow. Then DORIS scurries by holding a telegram.*

MICHAEL: I think it's scarier being in here!

Sissy: I know.

MICHAEL: They're like ghosts.

Sissy: I know. (*pause*) Michael.

> *She kisses him. Darkness. The funeral song swells in volume. End of Act One.*

ACT II

One
Michael

BEA: October 31, 1918.

CAST: Michael!

BEA: Everyone loved Michael. How it was that Michael caught the flu I guess we'll never know. But when he did he spoiled the whole reason for a town quarantine. The enemy was in our midst and it was everyone's favorite son.

So that day, the day that Michael went down …

SISSY: Michael?

BEA: It was in the middle of the field … mid-pitch. That stook hit the thresher side on, jammed the whole works and it ground to a halt. It even snapped a belt which whipped back and sliced Mickey Clark's face from ear to chin—lucky it didn't kill him. And everyone froze and looked at Michael. And Michael stared at that side-on stook, just reached towards it. Took one step. And in the gentle breeze he fell and lay as silent as the frozen thresher.

Stan said it was because he wasn't local—as if those germs just flew from infected towns looking for familiar faces. Stan said he'd be better off with his family in Yorkton. So the next train through had the surprising message to stop on the outskirts of town and Michael, weak and quiet, climbed aboard to be carried home.

Only, the train wasn't gone forty minutes when a message came from Yorkton. Michael's family was gone. A neighbour came to their house when she noticed there was no smoke from the chimney. And there inside, all in bed as though it was the middle of the night, was the whole family. Two brothers, three sisters, mother and father, all dead from the flu.

Sissy went to Doris and pleaded.

SISSY: Tell the train to send Michael back. There's no one to care for him there. We'll look after him here.

BEA: But no one would budge. And Sissy watched. And when the next westbound train passed through she saw Michael's face staring out a window. And when the next eastbound train came by he was on it too. And Sissy knew he was just riding 'til he got better—until they would let him off in Unity.

And the third time, Michael wasn't in the window. But the train slowed down a mile out of town and Michael was dropped off. Rolled in a gray blanket and dead. Sunna rode out, picked the body up and took him to her shed. And Sissy cried—the boy she loved was now in the arms of another woman.

SISSY: Beatrice!

BEATRICE cradles SISSY.

BEA: I'm sorry. I'm so sorry. Oh, Sissy.

> *SISSY breaks away and stares into BEATRICE's eyes.*
> *After a second she accepts the embrace of her sister.*

BEA: Oh, Sissy. My poor Sissy.

> *SISSY breaks away again and stares harder into*
> *BEATRICE's eyes.*

SISSY: You're happy.

BEA: Sissy?

SISSY: You're happy. All you've ever wanted was for me
to lose. To be like you. To be cold and angry
inside.

BEA: Sissy ...

SISSY: You're glad he's dead.

BEA: Oh, Sissy. I am not.

SISSY: You are.

BEA: No.

SISSY: Well, guess what. / So

BEA: No.

SISSY: am I. I'm happy he's dead too.

BEA: No, don't say that!

SISSY: And you can't take him away from me. Because
he's mine.

BEA: I ... Sissy, I ...

Sissy: I … Sissy, I … I, I, I, I, I. Too bad Beatrice. I'm not joining you there.

Bea: Where?

>   *Sissy exits.*

Bea: Sissy? Where?

Two
Doris

>   *At the telegraph office. The switchboard is ringing.*

Doris: Central.

Rose: No the doctor is sick.

Doris: Sorry the doctor is sick.

Rose: I know he's the doctor and he's sick! / He's a human being.

>   *Rose unplugs and quickly re-patches.*

Doris: No he's not answering his calls.

Rose: Central.

Doris: No I won't.

Rose: Oh hello Mernie.

Doris: Because it's pointless, / that's why.

Rose: Oh no, have you got it too?

Doris: Well I'll send / a message round,

Rose: The kids huh?

DORIS: but don't expect anything right / away. Okay.
Good-bye.

Switchboard continues to ring.

ROSE: No, it's been very busy. Everybody's calling for
him. And he's sick. (*to DORIS*) Doris!

DORIS: Central.

ROSE: Yes sick. That's right. / I know.

DORIS: Uh-huh.

ROSE: No the best thing is put them to bed, shut up
the windows tight. Keep that outside air from /
getting in.

DORIS: Uh-huh. Uh-huh.

ROSE: Uh-huh.

DORIS: Uh-huh.

ROSE: Uh-huh.

DORIS: Uh-huh.

ROSE: Uh-huh.

DORIS: Okay.

ROSE: Have you got camphor?

DORIS: Well don't go over there if they're all sick.
Everybody's / coming down with it.

ROSE: No, I don't think there's any left in town.
Mustard. Have you got mustard? That's the—
What's that?

DORIS: Uh-huh. Uh-huh.

DORIS starts unbuttoning her top.

ROSE: Well, I don't know if the trains will be stopping now.

DORIS: No, I'm listening.

ROSE: Yes. (*to DORIS*) What are you doing? (*back into phone*) I know, the quarantine's pointless now. Though I don't imagine that anyone would want to stop here now that they can.

DORIS collapses at her station.

ROSE: Doris!

Three
A Slow Leak

Darkness. Dripping.

HART: Sunna? (*pause*) Sunna? (*pause*) Out again. There's something dripping. You've got a leak somewhere young lady and I'm going to find it. Where's that coming from? You're losing precious fluids. What, I don't know. Drip, drip, drip. Must find the source.

Sound of him getting up and moving about the room.

Ooo, that's the wall. There's the stove and it's still going strong. A casket. Hello, sir. Oh, sorry, I mean ma'am. No, don't worry I didn't see anything. Another casket. Empty. Oh, this is one I did. Nice job on this Hart. Why, thank you. Okay, here's the bench. Drip, drip, drip, where are

you? Bottle of something. Jar of something else.
Those seem dry. Mmm. Funny smell there. Sour
milk? Empty jar.

Sound of glass breaking.

Aw, shit. What the hell was in there? Ow, glass.
Ew. That doesn't feel right.

Another crash.

Christ! Okay, okay, okay, let's get our story
straight. Cat snuck in, did cat things, blind man
sat helplessly by. Don't blame the blind.

HART finds his way back to his seat.

Casket, casket, stove, wall, and chair. Ah. Sorry
Sunna, you'll have to fix your own drip.

*There's a noise of someone moving, the sound of a
breath.*

HART: Who's there? Sunna?

VOICE: Shhhh.

HART: Who is it?

VOICE: She told me I could come.

HART: For me?

VOICE: No, for someone else.

Scene shifts.

Four
In Town

On the street two men wearing masks approach and pass each other.

MAN 1: (*turning back*) Fred?

MAN 2: Who's that?

MAN 1: Is that you Fred?

MAN 2: Ted?

MAN 1: Fred!

MAN 2: Ted! Geez, how are you?

They shake hands then wipe their palms on their trousers.

MAN 1: Oh, real good.

MAN 2: You done threshing then?

MAN 1: Oh yeah, you?

MAN 2: Oh, nearly, though.

MAN 1: Well, that'll be good then. It's like a ghost town down here.

MAN 2: Yup.

A woman wearing a mask passes by. They tip their hats.

MAN 1: Afternoon.

MAN 2: Who was that?

MAN 1: Wasn't that Gadfly's wife?

MAN 2: Was it?

MAN 1: I thought it was. Yep, it's quiet down here.

MAN 2: I read that this flu is uh … might be the Germans.

MAN 1: Is that right. I thought it might be the germs.

A little laugh.

MAN 2: No really, though, some secret weapon they planted on the coast.

MAN 1: Hmm. Now how did they manage to figure that out?

MAN 2: Well if they can get it going in one place on the coast with maybe one of those U-boats, then the rest sort of takes care of itself. / It's contagious.

MAN 1: I mean, but how did they figure out how to make a disease like that?

MAN 2: Oh, yeah, yeah, I don't know. They can do all sorts of things these days.

MAN 1: I guess that's true.

MAN 2: That poison, uh, gas.

MAN 1: Sure. Electricity and such.

MAN 2: Hmm?

MAN 1: It's amazing what can be done.

MAN 2: Oh, it sure is.

SISSY enters and as she passes gives them a hand-made flyer.

MAN 2: What's that say?

MAN 1: (*reading*) "End of the world to come.
Date set for late November.
Sissy Wilde speaks on the Apocalypse."

MAN 2: That's another epidemic.

MAN 1: What is?

MAN 2: Women speaking publicly.

MAN 1: Oh, yeah. There's that one ... What's that they
say about a dog walking on its hind legs?

MAN 2: I don't know.

MAN 1: Oh, it's something about that a woman talking
is like a dog on it's hind legs, or ... You know that
one?

MAN 2: No. You know Gadfly's got a smart little dog
there.

MAN 1: Gadfly does? Oh, yeah.

MAN 2: Yeah, a little Collie or something.

MAN 1: Is that what it is?

MAN 2: A little Collie I think. Smart little devil. Herds
like a son of a gun.

> SUNNA *walks by reading one of* SISSY's *pamphlets.*
> *The men nod to her.*

MAN 2: Who was that?

MAN 1: That was that Thorson girl.

MAN 2: Oh, yeah. Well I guess she's got her work cut
out for her now.

MAN 1: Yep. I suppose she's in the right business now.

MAN 2: If the world don't end.

MAN 1: Right. Well, better head for home.

MAN 2: Sure, then. Getting cold.

MAN 1: Oh, yeah. Yeah, could be a cold one.

> *They exit.*

Five
A Private Funeral

> *In the graveyard MARY kneels and places a small cross in the ground. In the background SUNNA is digging a grave. A body rests nearby. BEATRICE enters.*

MARY: Where's Sissy?

BEA: I don't know.

MARY: She said she'd come.

BEA: She's been acting strange. Let's start. We're not supposed to be here.

MARY: Ok. Um … Dearly beloved, we are gathered here today to pay respect to a brave soldier, a devoted son, and a dear friend who gave his life to protect us from the tyrant. Richard Stone. Richard died fighting for his country—the greatest sacrifice, the greatest love after the love of God. I place this cross so that we are ever reminded of his sacrifice and that we may always remember that he watches over us and protects us as was his choice to do when he went to war. Um … Beatrice, do you have anything to say?

BEA: She's watching us.

MARY: What?

BEA: Sunna's looking at us.

MARY: I don't care.

BEA: She's watching.

MARY: So is Richard.

BEA: Huh?

MARY: This is for Richard.

BEA: I know. (*pause*) Let's pray for a minute.

MARY: Okay.

They bow their heads.

BEA: November 10th, 1918. Mary and I gave Richard a funeral today. I prayed for his soul and Mary prayed he would watch over Unity and protect us from the flu, which struck me as odd, because it appears that the flu is what killed him. Like Michael, or others in town already. The difference being he died with a uniform on far away. Far enough away to imagine him carrying a flag as he coughed and sneezed his way across enemy lines. I thought about an extra big funeral when everyone else comes home and the flu is over. Sunna was in the graveyard, but didn't even stop digging a different grave during Richard's funeral. Mary and I worried about her even trying to stop us, which she sort of did by making us feel bad for being there. But we continued. I think I will write a poem for the soldiers when they get back.

MARY: I wrote a poem for Richard.

BEA: Ok.

MARY: (reading) Richard Stone you went to war
You were gone for one year and then one more
And one more year you stayed away
And we waited for you to return one day
But you were called to a greater place
And never more will we see your handsome face
Or your smile so bright or your thoughts so smart
But you will always live inside our hearts

BEA: (*aside*) I think I will write a poem for the soldiers when they get back. But it must be a very good poem—not just rhyming words and boring descriptions—so as not to embarrass them. It must contain words that scare you to speak them; a naked part of you to show them that their bravery has made you brave as well. Sissy came late to the funeral.

SISSY enters.

SISSY: Hi.

MARY: We already started.

BEA: I thought you weren't coming.

SISSY: So what are you doing?

MARY: Remembering Richard.

BEA: Praying.

MARY: I read a poem I wrote.

SISSY: Can I see?

MARY hands her the poem.

MARY: Don't step there!

SISSY: Why not?

MARY: That's the grave.

SISSY: Oh. (*pause*) It's a strange kind of funeral when the person isn't even here.

MARY: I think he is here.

SISSY: Oh. That's a nice poem. You should become a poet.

MARY: I think I could only write poems about Richard.

BEA: Do you have anything to say, Sissy?

SISSY: About what?

BEA: About Richard.

SISSY: I think Richard was swell. (*to MARY*) You should have been married and had a million babies.

MARY: He was going to …

Pause.

SISSY: It's cold. I'm giving my speech tomorrow night. Are you coming?

MARY: Where?

BEA: You can't.

SISSY: Behind the church. I'm going to do something special for Michael too. And I'll include Richard if you want.

MARY: In what?

SISSY: In what I'm doing.

MARY: What are you doing?

SISSY: Come tomorrow. Please.

> *SISSY holds MARY, hugs her, kisses her cheek where the tears have run.*

SISSY: I know.

> *MARY hugs SISSY.*

BEA: We should go.

MARY: I will always love you Richard. And I will never forget you.

> *MARY sprinkles dirt on the grave and she and SISSY exit. BEA hesitates, bends down and touches the grave.*
>
> *Suddenly SUNNA is behind her. BEATRICE jumps as she gets up and sees her. SUNNA touches the grave with the tip of her shovel.*

SUNNA: Who is it?

BEA: Nobody. It's not real.

SUNNA: You're pretending people are dying? There's real ones you can use.

BEA: No. We're not … We're just … Sorry.

> *BEA runs off. STAN appears carrying the body of his infant child. He walks over to where SUNNA has resumed digging and gently lays the child down. He helps her dig for a while, then suddenly breaks*

*down sobbing. SUNNA holds him and he suddenly
kisses her passionately on top of her mask.*

Six
A Call For Help

*A split scene between the telegraph office and
BEATRICE's home. DORIS lies convalescing while
ROSE speaks to BEATRICE.*

ROSE: Women are naturally good at taking care of
others. Men, even doctors, are weaker than
women. The town needs your help. There's a
natural strength that a woman gets when she's
helping others that protects her. You'll get the flu
faster by not helping.

BEA: Uh huh.

ROSE: You know, Beatrice, fear is the real killer. This
town was doing fine until people started to
believe they could catch the flu.

DORIS: It's a war.

ROSE: Yes, it's a war and we must be ready to fight.

BEA: It's a war.

ROSE: Yes, a war. There are so many families that need
you. And you know how to look after people.

BEA: I do?

ROSE: You've been looking after your father and sister
most of your life. I'd be out there, but it's
essential that I keep the telephones operating
and care for Doris. And we know how quickly she

92

would volunteer if she wasn't so ill. You can go to Doctor Lindsey's and take anything you need.

BEA: Okay.

Seven
Anatomy

SUNNA and STAN are silhouetted in lantern light. The soldier sits motionless in the corner. SUNNA wears a simple white wedding dress. STAN kisses SUNNA. SUNNA then begins to undress STAN. He does not hear her speak.

STAN: Oh, Sunna.

SUNNA: There are things that you can know. There are patterns you can find. Clues.

STAN: Oh ...

SUNNA: Most human bodies are the same. Draw two parallel lines down from the pupil of the eyes and you find the corners of the mouth. Tip of the thumb to the tip of the index finger is the length of the nose. Length of the nose is one-third the length of the face.

She touches his face: chin, brow, top of head.

One. Two. Three. The width of the eye is the distance between the eyes, which is the distance from where the ear joins the skull to the top of the ear. From the chin to the lower lip is twice that of the upper lip to the nose. From the wrist to the tip of the middle finger is the width of the

head. And the depth of the head? That's the ball
of the heel to the tip of the toe.

STAN: Sunna.

SUNNA: And half way between the hip and the knee is
where the longest finger touches when hanging
freely by the side.
Differences are only on the surface. Look closely
and you will see the same. The model is
consistent. Like triangles or circles, there's a
pattern. I look for patterns. Clues to keep me
going.

Fade to darkness.

Eight
A Sort of Salve

*In the mortuary BEATRICE is changing HART's
bandages. The Ukrainian funeral song is in the
distance. HART's back is to us as BEATRICE slowly
and tenderly unwraps the bandages. When she
finally uncovers his eyes she recoils momentarily,
then stares for a moment.*

HART: Pretty messy?

BEA: Oh...

HART: What's that music?

BEA: Uh, Ukrainians.

HART: (*laughs*) Oh, right.

BEA: What?

HART: Musical place—the Ukraine.

BEA: I don't know.

> *BEATRICE produces some ointment in a jar. She puts*
> *some on her fingers and moves towards his eyes,*
> *stops, withdraws, then tries again. Stops.*

HART: What's that smell?

BEA: Huh? Oh, I have something that might help. It's a
sort of salve for the skin. Um, for the burn. You
rub it on.

HART: Oh, sure. Let's have some.

BEA: Ok, just uh … give me your hands. Please.

> *HART extends his hands and BEA transfers the*
> *ointment from her fingers to his.*

BEA: Now just rub it around your eyes.

> *He does.*

HART: Quite a smell. That's nice singing.

BEA: I think it's a funeral.

HART: Oh yeah? How's this?

BEA: That's pretty good.

> *HART gropes for something to wipe his hands on.*
> *BEA looks too, but there's nothing around. She offers*
> *the hem of her dress. HART, without realizing what*
> *it is, wipes his hands vigorously, dabs his eyes and*
> *blows his nose. He starts gathering up the material*
> *trying to find its end.*

HART: Wow, a big hanky.

BEA quickly snatches it away embarrassed. Silence.
BEA puts the ointment away.

HART: (*figures it out*) Oh! (*pause*) Oh ... sorry.

BEA: It's okay.

HART: I thought ... I didn't ... Oh, that's really terrible of me.

BEA: No, it's fine. (*small laugh*) Big hanky. Here's a fresh bandage.

She bandages his eyes.

HART: Ah, that's good.

They sit. Silence.

HART: Yep. (*sings*) Dee diddely dee.

Pause.

HART: It's nice to have company. The living sort.

BEA: (*pause*) I've got the newspaper from Saskatoon. Would you like me to read it to you?

HART: Oh that sounds nice.

BEA: They have this section where they write stories of Canadian bravery.

HART: War stories?

BEA: Yes.

HART: No.

BEA: They're always quite good.

HART: No, I don't want to hear any!

BEA: Oh, but—

HART: I said no!

BEA: I—

HART: They're not true.

BEA: They're not?

HART: No.

BEA: I'm sure they wouldn't / write them if …

HART: They're always some stupid story about some stupid guy who's run out of ammunition and wounded in every part of his body, who takes over command after his captain's been killed and somehow runs a mile into enemy territory where, with only a rock and comb, manages to kill seven hundred Germans and take an entire battalion prisoner, who he marches right across the English Channel while getting them all to sing God Save the King. Right? But, they're never about the guy sitting in a trench with his lousy jammed up standard issue rifle that has only fired one shot before busting with his head between his knees and his pants full of his own shit because he's been there for three days in the same position between the corpses of a couple of guys who looked up when he said "Heads Down" and he's wondering if the captain who he last saw running the other way was really just going for more supplies or is he dead or is he what or is he just the only one who had any brains.

BEA: Oh.

HART: That's all. So I don't like those stories. (*pause*) Is there anything else in that paper?

BEA: Well ... um ... Not much ... else ... Just some
      other little news and advertisements.

HART: For what?

BEA: Oh, you know, medicine, biscuits, uh stove, ladies
      fashions, / automobiles ...

HART: Yeah read me those. Ladies fashions. What's
      new this fall?

BEA: Ladies fashions?

HART: Yeah. What are they wearing now?

BEA: Well, here's one for hats—quite a few hats—and I
      think they don't look very practical ... and right
      next is silk ... uh ... silk underwear ...

HART: Mmmm ...

      Scene shifts.

Nine
A Fire

*Sissy stands in the night air with a lantern. She
reads from the Bible.*

SISSY: "And behold a pale horse, and he that sat upon
      him, his name was death and hell followed him.
      And power was given to him over the four parts
      of the earth, to kill with sword, with famine, and
      with death, and with the beasts of the earth!"
      Members, we are less than a month away from
      the prophesied date and we will soon be
      released. Six thousand years are up. Michael, like
      the lamb, you were the first. Clearing the way for

us all. A fire, a fire you wanted. So tonight, a fire for Michael, for life at the edge of death, at the edge of eternity.

Flames rise.

Ten
Telegraph Office

ROSE is at the switchboard. DORIS is resting.

ROSE: Central. Hello Stan. Good lord, where? Oh my lord. Just a second.

She rises and looks out her window.

DORIS: Now what has he done?

ROSE: (*to DORIS*) Shh! (*to STAN*) Yes I can see the flames from here. Well who can I call? We'll never get enough people together. As long as you're safe … Call who? Wilde's? What for? She did? Why? Oh my lord, she didn't! Why would she do such a thing? That's a desecration … I'll call and I'll come right down.

Eleven
The Mortuary

BEATRICE alone.

BEA: November 11th, 1918. Still no trains into Unity. Father rode Blister to Saskatoon for winter work. He said he wasn't worried about the flu—too many other people to pick on in the big city. He

99

said he wasn't worried about us. He knew that I could take care of things. When I told him that I would make sure that Sissy went back to school when they opened again he said it didn't really matter. The girl knows too much already. I didn't tell him about Sissy wanting to give a speech about the Bible. And I didn't tell him that I wished *I* could be the one to ride away—wished I could leave instead of being left behind. Last night, I was woken by a call from Rose.

In the mortuary.

STAN: How the hell could you think of doing that to another human being?

SISSY: It's what he wanted.*

SUNNA: He was dead.

STAN: *You destroyed my property! (*to SUNNA*) What?

SUNNA: He was dead, is all.

STAN: What difference does that make? (*back to SISSY*) It was my property! You've committed some serious crimes here.

BEATRICE enters.

BEA: Sissy! What's happened?

STAN: Where's your father?

BEA: Saskatoon.

STAN: Saskatoon?*

BEA: Yes, he left—

ROSE: (*entering*) Now what's going on?

SISSY: *He works at the sawmill there after / harvest is done.

STAN: Quiet!

BEA: (*to SISSY*) What happened?*

ROSE: (*to BEATRICE*) You shouldn't be here.

STAN: *She stole a body from here / and burned it

SISSY: (*to ROSE*) She shouldn't? And you should?

STAN: on my haystack. / (*to SISSY*) I said quiet, you!

ROSE: God help us!

BEA: Sissy!*

SISSY: Michael wanted it!

HART: *Excuse me—

BEA: Sissy ...

STAN: I have horses!

ROSE: What's the matter with your horses? / (*covering her nose as she gets close to the body*) Oh my lord!

STAN: Nothing, but they'll starve this winter / thanks to this

SISSY: They won't starve!

STAN: girl here. They will without feed!*

SISSY: It's the end of—

ROSE: *What happened to the boy?*

SISSY: Beatrice?

HART: Excuse me—

STAN: *She set him on fire.

ROSE: Oh my lord! Where is he?

SUNNA: (*referring to a corpse under a sheet*) Here.

SISSY: Beatrice, please.

ROSE: (*looking under sheet*) Oh, my lord Jesus Christ!

STAN: See!

SISSY: It's worse because they pulled him off! / You should have left him!

STAN: Don't you dare blame us you evil bitch of a whore!

ROSE: Stan!

STAN: She destroyed my feed!

SISSY: Not all of it!

ROSE: What about the boy!*

STAN: That's another thing altogether.

SUNNA: *I'll bury him tomorrow.

SISSY: You don't touch him. I'll bury him tomorrow.*

SUNNA: Fine.

STAN: *You'll do no such thing! / We'll end up

SISSY: You can't tell me—

ROSE: I don't know why he wasn't buried before!*

STAN: losing the whole town. God knows what—(*to BEATRICE*) Goddammit girl! Your father will pay me for that lost hay!

102

BEA: I'm sure we'll be able—

SUNNA: *She wanted to see him.

HART: Hello! Excuse me! If I may say ... Excuse me, sorry, but if I may say, Sissy may have been trying to help you all.

STAN: What?

HART: That boy died of the flu. The body carries germs. Burning it may have been wise, in a way. / I'm not saying it's all right, really, but—

ROSE: You don't treat a human body like some pile of rubbish! / No it's definitely not all right!

SISSY: Rubbish? It was a funeral!

STAN: (*to* BEA) What's wrong with your family?

BEA: Nothing!

HART: Sir, be fair. / These girls are very kind.

ROSE: We would have been better off if you never came here.*

STAN: Leave him alone!

BEA: *This has nothing to do with him!

ROSE: He brought this flu!

BEA: He's not even sick!

HART: Is she talking about me?

STAN: Rose, he didn't do anything!

ROSE: I'm not blaming the girl, Stan, although it's certainly doing her no harm with people sick and dying.

103

STAN: You keep your mouth shut about her!

ROSE: She's just like her uncle was. No sense of—and then bringing in someone who's been in the middle of an epidemic.

HART: She didn't bring me in! She didn't want me here!

STAN: Well why the hell did you come?

SISSY: He wanted a fire!

> *Pause.*

HART: Me?

SISSY: Michael! Michael wanted a fire! I was doing it for him! No one would help him so why do you care? (*to* ROSE) You! Rubbish? He was thrown dead off the train like rubbish! Nobody complained then! Now you're upset? I won't have him stuffed underground with no one noticing or caring. Even when you knew there was no one for him at home you wouldn't let him back! And I wasn't trying to stop the flu either! I hope you all catch it and you all die!

> *Underneath the end of her line the phone the phone begins to sound a strange pattern of rings.*

ROSE: Shhh! Emergency ring! (*she picks up the phone*) Doris? Yes? Speak up. Oh my lord, oh my lord. (*she hangs up*) Telegram. It's over. The war is over. It's victory.

> *Silence for a moment. Suddenly everybody cheers and hugs. SISSY joins in the rejoicing and is included by all. HART is pulled into the fray. The group suddenly stops and there is silence except for a howling wind that has come up. Everyone slowly with-*

draws from each other and masks are produced and donned. Lantern light flickers, then darkness.

Twelve
V-Day Dance

BEA: November 13, 1918. Last night I slept so deeply. Last night I didn't dream. I awoke to the sound of the train whistle as the first train pulled into the station since the town was quarantined.

MARY: (*she clears her throat with a little cough*) Oh, sorry. The Victory Day Dance. Welcome. Under special provisions, the town by-law prohibiting public gatherings has been amended to allow for this celebration dance in honour of the end of the war. However, there are certain and specific rules: masks must be worn at all times, the dance will only last 1 hour and thirty minutes, and band members playing brass instruments are kindly asked to not empty their spit valves onto the bandstand or dance hall floor. Thank you. Also, dance partners wishing to dance must remain one yard apart at all times. A very special welcome home to Unity's own returning war heroes: Alan McCaw and Glen Brambley.

> *BEATRICE, SISSY, and MARY stand separately. Shadows of dancers flicker about the stage. GLEN stands in uniform isolated in a shaft of light. BEATRICE tries to get up the nerve to approach him, when SISSY beats her to the punch. SISSY and GLEN dance a waltz without touching each other. Over time their steps become more complicated and they are perfectly in synch. Meanwhile BEATRICE watches*

in frustration until she can't take it anymore. GLEN dips SISSY still without touching her. When she's fully extended backwards BEATRICE screams out.

BEA: Glen!

SISSY falls.

BEA: Glen!

GLEN: Hi?

BEA: Hi. Sorry.

SISSY: What are you doing?

BEA: You don't mind Sissy. Sorry.

GLEN: Who is that?

BEA: It's me … Beatrice. Beatrice Wilde.

GLEN: Oh. Oh, hi. How are you?

BEA: Fine. (*to SISSY*) Get up!

SISSY: I was waiting for a hand.

BEA: You don't / need a hand.

GLEN: I'm sorry. Let me help you—

He reaches down and helps SISSY up.

VOICE: One yard apart!

GLEN: (*pulling back*) Ooops.

SISSY: Thanks.

BEA: I don't mean to interrupt, but—

GLEN: That's okay.

SISSY: I'm going for punch.

BEA: Okay.

GLEN: Thanks for the dance.

SISSY: Save another one for me. You're pretty good.

> *She exits.*

BEA: How are you?

GLEN: I'm really good. How are you?

BEA: Fine.

GLEN: Well, great. You surprised me there.

BEA: I'm sorry. I just wanted to tell you—

VOICE: One yard apart!

BEA: Oh. I just wanted to tell you how proud … we all are of you.

GLEN: Oh, thanks.

BEA: And we're really glad you're home.

GLEN: Oh me too.

BEA: You are?

VOICE: One yard apart over there!

GLEN: (*to the chaperone*) Sorry! (*to BEATRICE*) Do you want to go outside?

BEA: Uh … (*pause*) yes.

GLEN: Great! Let's cool off, as they say.

BEA: Sure.

BEATRICE hesitates looking back at SISSY and MARY and then exits with GLEN. Suddenly they are outside in the night air.

GLEN: Yeah, it's good to be home.

BEA: It is?

GLEN: It was a long time.

BEA: I know. It was.

GLEN: Yeah, and you begin to forget things.

BEA: You did? Like what?

GLEN: Oh little things. The look of town, the feeling of being here, people ...

BEA: Does it seem different?

GLEN: Well, then you come back and it all just seems like yesterday. Nothing's changed / and what you

BEA: No, it hasn't.

GLEN: thought you had forgotten is all there again.

BEA: Oh, that's good. You're just like I remembered.

GLEN: Yeah?

BEA: Well, you seem more ... Well ... I don't know ... You look ... (*she mumbles*) Well you look very handsome.

GLEN: What?

BEA: Oh, you just look nice in your uniform.

GLEN: Oh, thanks.

BEA: It must have been hard to come back to little
Unity after seeing the rest of the world.

GLEN: No, it wasn't hard at all. What I saw of the world
wasn't all that great.

BEA: Oh.

GLEN: I'm looking forward to getting back on the farm
and settling down.

BEA: Really?

GLEN: Sure. Hey, can I show you something special?

BEA: Yes.

He produces a wool sock.

BEA: (*gasps*) Oh. I recognize that.

GLEN: You do?

BEA: Yes. I ... I knit that sock. (*pause*) And another one
just like it.

GLEN: No.

BEA: Yes.

GLEN: You're teasing me.

BEA: No. I know it's mine. See this? This is something
special I'd do. I'm sure no one else would do it
just like that.

GLEN: Wow. That is very strange.

BEA: I know.

GLEN: It's amazing!

BEA: I know!

GLEN: You knit this sock?

BEA: Yes!

GLEN: And I got it!

BEA: Yes!

GLEN: It's amazing!

BEA: I know!

GLEN: Because this sock is very important to me.

BEA: It is?

GLEN: Yep. It kept me going through the war.

BEA: Really? How?

GLEN: 'Cause it protected what was most dear to me.

BEA: What?

> *GLEN produces a locket rolled in the sock, opens it and shows BEATRICE a picture.*

GLEN: This is my wife.

BEA: Wife?

GLEN: Her name is Alice. I met her in London before going to fight. We got married just before I left and I carried this picture with me the whole time over. I'm sure I would have busted it without this sock. It's a real great sock. She's coming to Unity. She should be here in the spring.

BEA: Oh. She's pretty.

GLEN: Oh, she's real swell. You'd like her, I'd bet.

BEA: I'd bet.

GLEN: Well, Beatrice Wilde. I owe you.

> *GLEN moves to hug BEATRICE. He suddenly sneezes, pulls back, laughs. The threshing machine roars. Darkness.*

Thirteen
Mary

> *BEATRICE is caring for SISSY and MARY who have both fallen ill .*

BEA: November 14, 1918. Mary not feeling well after dance ... too many spinning waltzes? Laughed at that. Ha Ha. November 15. Water to McCaw's farm ... little snow, ground's freezing. November 16. Sissy complains of being tired. What from, not sure. November 17. Soup to Mitchell's, O'Hara's, and Dent's (pretty cold when I got to the Dent's). November 18. The war is supposed to be over, but the war is still on. I don't know what to do.

> *BEATRICE sponges MARY's head, SISSY lies in bed looking at a newspaper.*

SISSY: See this? It's coming for sure. President Wilson of United States. Born 1856, came to power in 1912, reigned 6 years, his age 62. Add those numbers up and it's 3836. Divide by two: 1918. President Poincarré of France. Born 1860, came to power 1913, reigned 5 years, aged 58. Add it up—3836. Divide by two: 1918. It works for the King of England, Italy, the Czar, even the Mikado.

BEA: What about Canada? Does it work for Borden?

SISSY: It doesn't have him. I don't think it would change anything if it worked for Borden or not. But it works for the King of Servia! / Just a few more days left.

> *MARY begins to convulse and choke.*

BEA: Mary! Mary! I don't think she can breathe!

SISSY: Call the doctor.

BEA: Sissy, Doctor Lindsey is dead.

SISSY: Well do something! Call somebody!

> *BEATRICE grabs the telephone and rings over and over for help. No response. MARY stops coughing.*

BEA: No answer!

SISSY: I think she's okay now.

BEA: Mary? Mary?

SISSY: Is she okay?

BEA: November 18, 1918. P.S. (*pause*) P.S.

> *BEATRICE stops, then covers MARY with a sheet.*

Fourteen
A Dry Cough

> *HART is nailing the lid onto a coffin. He breaks into a coughing fit. SUNNA enters wearing the wedding dress dyed black and carrying some dried*

flowers. Throughout his monologue, she weeps silently.

HART: This reminds me of something that happened some time ago in Halifax. Our neighbour, old Mr. Morris, passed on and after the funeral they had the usual procession up the hill to the cemetery. Now this hill goes straight out of down town and is quite steep. Well, part way up the hill the carriage carrying the late Mr. Morris broke away from the horses and started rolling backwards down the hill. That carriage rolled past his wife and children, past the congregation, and kept on rolling. Now that road is as straight as an arrow and the carriage just kept on going with everybody chasing after it. It rolled right to the bottom of the hill and right into downtown and it kept on going. It seemed like nothing would stop it. Finally it rolled right to the end of the street where the drug store stood. And it kept on going. It rolled right through the front window of the drug store, across the room and right into the counter at a tremendous speed. Well the casket popped open, and the body of Old Mr. Morris suddenly sat up and said, "Hey, Apothecary, can you give me something to stop this coffin?"

HART bursts into another coughing fit.

SUNNA: You're sick?

HART: No, just dust in my throat I think.

SUNNA: Sit down.

HART collapses onto the cot.

HART: Are you wearing a dress?

113

SUNNA: Yes.

HART: (*holding out his hand*) May I?

> *SUNNA guides his hand over the material.*

HART: It's nice. (*pause*) Sunna, I'm sorry about Stan.

> *SUNNA places the flowers on the coffin.*

SUNNA: It's all right. I don't think he was ever very happy.

HART: I wonder if he knew that.

SUNNA: You're right. You did a good job on the casket.

HART: Thanks. What happened to that fire?

SUNNA: What?

HART: Could you stoke it up a bit? It's getting pretty cold in here.

> *SUNNA touches his forehead.*

SUNNA: Why don't you lie down for a while?

HART: I'll help you move Stan outside.

SUNNA: I'll manage. You should rest for awhile. It's later than you think.

HART: Time makes no difference. It's always just after dark for me.

> *He curls up and SUNNA covers him with a blanket.*

Fifteen
New Iceland

BEATRICE is sponging SISSY's head. SISSY is delirious.

SISSY: Am I dying?

BEA: Of course not. You just have to rest.

SISSY: I don't want to die yet.

BEA: You won't. They say lots of rest and you'll be fine. The worst part is over after the first couple of days.

SISSY: What day is it?

BEA: November 23rd.

SISSY: Just a few more days until the end.

BEA: Oh, Sissy.

SISSY: I can't die before the end. It would be so embarrassing. I formed a club. I gave a presentation. I want to see the end. Bea. Oh, no. This is it. Bea, don't let her take me.

BEA: Oh, Sissy. Don't talk like that.

SISSY: Don't let her take me!

BEA: Who?

SISSY: The angel of death.

BEA: Sissy. You're just dreaming. You're hot. There's no one here but me.

SISSY: Behind you.

BEATRICE turns and jumps at the sight of SUNNA, who has entered wearing black and holding a scythe.

SUNNA: Is this yours?

BEA: What are you doing here?*

SUNNA: It was in the yard.

SISSY: *She's come for me.

BEA: Shh! No she hasn't.

SISSY: (*throwing her pillow at SUNNA*) Get back reaper!

BEA: Lie down! (*to SUNNA*) What do you want?

SUNNA: It'll rust in the rain.

SISSY: Get her Beatrice. Watch out for the blade.

BEA: Shhh. (*to SUNNA*) Why are you here?*

SUNNA: I need to—

SISSY: *She's here to do battle. Hit her with this.

SISSY produces a polished wooden dildo that lay under her pillow.

BEA: (*taking it*) What is that?

SISSY: A weapon!

SUNNA: That's a pretend penis.

BEA: (*she drops it*) Sissy!

SISSY: Hit her with it! Hit her with it!

BEA: No! Sissy, quiet!

SISSY: Fight for me Bea!

BEA: (*to SUNNA*) Can you go away? You're upsetting her.*

SUNNA: Please—

SISSY: *No, words are no good. You've got to use the stick.

BEA: (*to SISSY*) Shhh! (*to SUNNA*) Get out!

SUNNA: Please—Sissy, I'm not here for you. I need your sister.

SISSY: Oh. Oh, Beatrice, it's you she wants. I'm too weak to fight for you. I'll see you on the other side.

BEA: Sissy! (*to SUNNA*) What do you want?

SUNNA: I need your help. Stan got the flu / and then he gave it to Hart—

BEA: You know lot's of people are sick.

SUNNA: But I can't care for him.

BEA: Why not?

SUNNA: Uh—

BEA: Because you're too busy digging graves?

SUNNA: I have to work.

BEA: You can't care for him because you're too busy making money off of everybody else's death.

SUNNA: I'll pay you.

BEA: I'm not a vulture. I don't want to make money from other people's suffering. / I'm already looking after five farms!

117

SUNNA: I have nobody. And neither does he. He shouldn't have to die for being alone.

BEA: Then look after him.

SUNNA: I can't. I have work to do.

BEA: Graves to dig.

SUNNA: Yes.

BEA: Then I guess you're going to have to dig one more.

SUNNA: I thought you would care.

BEA: Me? What about you?

SUNNA: That's why I'm here. That's why I'm asking for your help. You're the only nurse in town.

BEA: I'm not a nurse.

SUNNA: But it's what you're doing.

BEA: I'm trying to help win the war. What are you trying to do? You help the enemy.

SUNNA: War?

BEA: The war against the flu.

SUNNA: I don't have a war. Or an enemy. But this is my work. And it's all I have. It's what I can do.

BEA: What's more important—Stan or digging holes?

SUNNA: Stan? No, Stan's dead. It's Hart that's sick now. He asked for you.

BEA: Hart? He did? Oh … Oh, poor Stan. When?

SUNNA: Two days ago. It came very quickly. (*pause*) I don't belong here. (*pause*) Nobody wants to do what I do. (*pause*) Hart has no one. And I don't know how to help him. But I see you are good at this. I'm not asking for me. Hart isn't mine. He's by himself. Just like me. And that's why I have to do my work. It's all I have. I'm saving money. I want to go home.

BEA: Home?

Pause.

SUNNA: Iceland.

SISSY: (*who's been drifting in and out of consciousness*) Silly. People don't go to Iceland. They leave Iceland and come here.

BEA: Shhh. Sissy.

SUNNA: Because they think it will be better here.

BEA: Maybe it is.

SUNNA: But maybe it's just big and empty and full of people trying to make believe they're somewhere that they're not. And having children who grow up never knowing what this place really is or what the place was that their parents pretend it to be. And more and more lost they are until the emptiness is all they know of home. I don't want that home. I think they meant well by sending me here. How were they to know there was no such place as New Iceland?

SISSY: Maybe they don't want you back.

BEA: Shh.

SUNNA: I'm not asking for me.

Silence.

SUNNA: I dressed Mary in white. And gave her back the wheat shafts to hold. (*pause*) Help him if you can.

SUNNA exits.

Sixteen
Hart and Bea

The mortuary. HART is lying amidst the bodies. BEATRICE enters.

HART: Sunna?

BEA: No. It's Beatrice. I heard you weren't well.

HART: Where's Sunna.

BEA: In the graveyard.

HART: She's dead?

BEA: No. She's just digging graves.

HART: Who's dead?

BEA: Lot's of people.

HART: Me too, soon enough, I guess.

BEA: No. You just have to rest.

HART: What colour are my feet?

BEA: What?

HART: What colour are my feet? I heard a doctor on the train in Montreal say that when the feet turn black there's no hope.

> BEATRICE *lifts the sheet revealing his feet. They're black.*

BEA: Your feet are fine.

HART: I can see the end.

BEA: See the end? Please. You're delirious. You're blind; you can't see the end. Just rest.

> *She sponges his forehead.*

HART: Something has happened.

BEA: What?

HART: I think it's the war.

BEA: Yes, it's over now.

HART: Yes, and something big has happened. A hole.

BEA: What?

HART: I guess it's when there's so much traffic between this world and the next the space between them is stretched out of shape. The wrong people fall over to the other side and angels slip out of heaven and wander around down here bumping into things.

BEA: Hmm?

HART: It's dark down here. Heaven's much brighter and your eyes get used to it. Angels are a clumsy lot if they end up back here. Lot's of accidents. Broken things. People pushed by mistake into the other world.

BEA: And are you an angel?

HART: Are you?

BEA: No, I'm just a girl.

HART: The last girl I saw was in France.

BEA: A nurse?

HART: A prostitute.

BEA: Oh.

HART: She was very pretty.

BEA: Oh.

HART: Very pretty.

BEA: Well, I suppose that was good for business.

HART: She was my first.

BEA: Well.

HART: She went to blow out the candles, but I wanted to see.

BEA: Oh?

HART: I said, "Don't blow out the candles." And she said, "Quoi?" Just like that. "Quoi?" That's funny, huh? "Quoi?" I wanted to see her. And then I realized she couldn't see me.

BEA: She couldn't see?

HART: Me. I was invisible to her. But I couldn't do it without being seen. Without her knowing it was me.

BEA: You weren't ... ashamed?

HART: Only if I was invisible. I had to do something to make myself be seen. So I placed her hand on my heart and thought really hard, "See this." And her hand on my mouth—again, "See." And the strangest thing was, I began to see myself through her hand. My face, my chest. And then I knew I had never seen myself before.

BEA: But—

HART: No, never. And I wondered if this pretty girl had ever seen herself before. So I placed my hand on her face—"See this." On her neck—"There." Her breasts—"These." Her belly—"Here." And light seemed to flood the room—much more than a candle. And there, her clothes fell away and then I looked down, got down on my knees, and ... I guess it was there that I lost my sight.

BEA: There?

HART: There. The last I ever saw.

BEA: You went blind by looking at ... her—

Pause.

BEA: You don't think it was perhaps the gas attack?

HART: No. I don't think so.

BEA: Well, I don't think looking at that can make you blind.

HART: No?

BEA: Well, I'm sure you shouldn't have been looking there, but—

HART: I saw through to the other side.

BEA: Huh?

HART: And the next day we went to battle. And I thought I saw. I thought I saw the guns, the fire, the men falling around me, and the gas, the green-yellow fog ... but it was a dream. I had already seen the other side and could see no more. Are you there?

BEA: Yes. Here.

> *She sponges him some more.*

HART: Have you ever seen yourself?

BEA: I ... don't know.

HART: Would you like to?

BEA: Yes.

HART: I think that's good.

> *She watches him breathe for a while. Then slowly she undoes her mask and lets it drop. She softly kisses him on the lips. Very bright light.*

Seventeen
A Vision

> *BEATRICE is on an empty road. She holds her diary. SUNNA appears from the distance walking towards her carrying a cross for a grave on one shoulder and her shovel in the opposite hand.*

BEA: Sunna.

SUNNA: Hello Beatrice. Lost?

BEA: Yes. I don't know … I've been out here for hours. I don't know where I am. I'm supposed to be helping … someone. Which way is Unity?

SUNNA: It's okay. You know the war is over?

BEA: It is? Yes. Yes, I knew that.

SUNNA: You've done a lot Beatrice.

BEA: It doesn't feel like it.

SUNNA: Well, you have.

BEA: Thank you for taking care of Mary.

> *Silence.*

BEA: Are you going home now?

SUNNA: Yes.

BEA: Can I follow you?

SUNNA: No.

BEA: Oh.

SUNNA: Just keep going this way.

BEA: Okay. I'm all turned around out here.

SUNNA: I know.

BEA: But I'm glad I saw you.

> *Distant singing is heard.*

BEA: What is that music?

SUNNA: You're tired.

BEA: I am.

SUNNA: Why don't you rest?

BEA: Okay. I'll just watch the singers for a while.

> BEATRICE *lies down. A funeral procession passes by out of which* SISSY *steps taking* BEATRICE's *diary from her.*

Eighteen
The Apocalypse

> SISSY *sits by the body of* BEATRICE *who is laid out on the bed.* SUNNA *stands nearby.*

SISSY: Oh, Beatrice. "And in those days men shall seek death, and shall not find it: and they shall desire to die, and death shall fly from them."

> SISSY *picks up* BEATRICE's *diary and reads the final entry while* SUNNA *examines the corpse and measures it.*

SISSY: "November 28, 1918. Today was the day the world was to come to an end. A relief for some, a disappointment for others that it in fact still continues much like it did yesterday or the day before. My sister has recovered quickly from the flu. She's always been a little faster at most things than the normal person. I'm a little under the weather, but not needed so much right now, so it's not so inconvenient. We won the war, so quite a few people feel a little bit relieved about all of that. And winter is here. A promise of darkness and cold for some time. But for me the world is brighter than it's ever been before. I kissed a boy

a few days back. I still feel him on my lips. He was very,
very … "

The entry stops there. SISSY closes the book; touches BEA.

SISSY: (*softly*) Lucky.

Drums like gunfire are heard.

A Song

SONG:

And this is your birthday

Your day of reckoning
This is your coming of age

Bitter victory
Bloody glory
There is no teary-eyed homecoming story
This is our only home
Oh, Canada!

And Children rise!
Children rise!
Take your place among men
And women rise
Women rise
Take your place among soldiers, then

It's everybody's fight
It's everybody's victory
It's everybody's misery
We've overcome
We've overcome

And out of darkness
For it's ever dawn
A hundred years of progress
A Century for us

Oh, Canada!
Oh, Canada!
Oh—

Curtain.